8-28-64

$3.00

1944-6-5

The Idea of Revelation
in Recent Thought

NUMBER 7

Bampton Lectures in America

DELIVERED AT

COLUMBIA UNIVERSITY

1954

The Idea of Revelation
in Recent Thought

by JOHN BAILLIE

Columbia University Press NEW YORK

Preface

The chapters which follow represent the Bampton Lectures in America delivered at Columbia University in July, 1954. Since the lectures had to be prepared on very short notice, I was allowed the privilege of revising, and at the same time measurably expanding, them before submitting them for publication. The task I had set myself in the first instance was the comparatively humble one of attempting to survey the considerable body of recent thought and writing concerning revelation. What I had in mind might be described as an extended review. If in the event I have written something in the nature of an independent essay, I have certainly done no more than that. Had a full systematic treatment been intended, many other questions must necessarily have been raised.

Not all the recent books which were in my mind or in my hand as I wrote have been specifically cited in the text, but most of them are in the list which I have appended.

I am very sensible of the honour conferred upon me by the Trustees of Columbia University in appointing me to this Lectureship; and I am most grateful to President

Grayson Kirk and to Secretary Richard Herpers, as well as to President van Dusen of Union Theological Seminary, for their kindness and helpfulness in connection with the delivery of the lectures. To the large audience which crowded the rotunda of Low Memorial Library on those sultry summer evenings I owe a further debt of gratitude for their most indulgent hearing.

My friend, Professor J. Y. Campbell of Westminster College, Cambridge, and formerly of Yale University, has been good enough to read the proofs for me, and I have greatly profited from his comments. My brother, the late Professor Donald M. Baillie of St. Andrews University, read my original typescript shortly before his death and suggested many most necessary emendations.

JOHN BAILLIE

Edinburgh, Scotland
February, 1956

Contents

The Idea of Revelation
in Recent Thought

I: Historical Reminder

What do we mean by revelation? It is a question to which much hard thinking and careful writing are being devoted in our time, and there is a general awareness among us that it is being answered in a way that sounds very differently from the traditional formulations. What I have in mind to do is to define as precisely as possible the position which has now emerged, and I shall do it very largely by means of a study of the more recent contributions to the subject, attempting to discriminate between them where they conflict, and pulling together as much of them as appears acceptable. But let us first, in this chapter, remind ourselves of the stages by which the change has come about. It is a story which has often been told and may be resumed very briefly.

REVELATION IN SEVENTEENTH- AND EIGHTEENTH-CENTURY THOUGHT

Throughout the greater part of Christian history the question was not thought to be a difficult one. It was answered in terms of the distinction between revealed and

natural or rational knowledge, and an intelligent schoolboy could have told you what that distinction was. He
would have explained to you that there are two sharply
contrasted ways in which men have gained knowledge of
God and things divine—by the unaided exercise of their
own powers of thinking, and by direct communication
from God Himself. If instead of the schoolboy you had
consulted a learned theologian, you would have received
very much the same answer. St. Thomas Aquinas, in the
thirteenth century, would tell you on the one hand of "an
ascent, by the natural light of reason, through created
things to the knowledge of God," and on the other of "a
descent, by the mode of revelation, of divine truth which
exceeds the human intellect, yet not as demonstrated to
our sight but as a communication delivered for our belief
(*quasi sermone prolata ad credendum*)." [1] If your theologian belonged to an earlier period of the Middle Ages
instead of to the thirteenth century, he would perhaps en-
courage you to hope that most of our available knowledge
of God could be approached from either direction, but
St. Thomas and most of his successors would carry the distinction, not only to the two ways of knowing, but to
the respective areas of knowledge to which these were
able to conduct us; holding that there were many truths
given by revelation to which reason could not attain at
all. But where all were agreed was that, whether or not
the *scibile* covers the same ground as the *credibile, scire*
remains an entirely different process from *credere.* Our
schoolboy might thus reflect that the two ways whereby
men had acquired divine knowledge correspond very
closely to the two ways, so familiar to himself, of becoming

[1] *Summa contra Gentiles,* IV, chap. i.

possessed of the answer to a mathematical problem—
working it out for himself or taking it on trust from his
master or his textbook; except that he had here to do
with some theorems which he could not possibly work out
for himself, and that the authority from whom he took
the answers on trust could, unlike his master or his textbook, be shown to be incapable of error.

This way of defining revelation as communicating a
body of knowledge, some part at least of which could be
independently obtained, or at least verified, by "the light
of reason and nature," while the remainder was supple-
mental to what could be so obtained or verified, was long
to remain unchallenged. For the most part the terms of
the distinction were as readily accepted after the close of
the Middle Ages as during the course of them, as readily
outside Roman orthodoxy as within it. Even as late as
1867 a Calvinist theologian would be writing:

We define reason to be man's natural faculty of reaching the
truth, including his understanding, heart, conscience and experience, acting under natural circumstances, and without
any supernatural assistance. And we define faith, on the other
hand, to be the assent of the mind to truth, upon the testimony of God, conveying knowledge to us through supernatural channels. . . . Reason establishes the fact that God
speaks, but when we know what He says, we believe it because He says it.[2]

What was disturbed after the break-up of the Middle
Ages was not the terms of the distinction, but the balance
of emphasis as between them. This happened in two opposite ways. The rationalists of the seventeenth and eight-

[2] A. A. Hodge, *Outlines of Theology*, ed. by W. H. Goold (London,
Edinburgh, 1863), pp. 49f.

eenth centuries, though rarely quarrelling with the traditional understanding of reason and revelation (so that
there was little or no dispute at this point between them
and the orthodox apologists who tried to answer them),
came to place almost the whole of their reliance on the
former, gradually edging the latter out of its former pride
of position. The more extreme of them went so far as to
deny that any revelation had been vouchsafed to us, as-
serting that in fact we have no knowledge of divine things
save what is discoverable by our own unaided powers.
Others, and perhaps the majority, were content to argue
that such supernatural revelation as had been given,
through the prophets and through Christ and His apostles,
could be nothing more than what they called a "republica-
tion," for the benefit of weaker minds, of truths which a
sufficiently sustained and honest exercise of reason could
know independently, or even of truths which formerly
had been known but afterwards variously obscured and
overlaid by superstition. Either way of it, the rationalists
succeeded to their own satisfaction in clearing the whole
ground of possible debate for the free exercise of their
own speculation and especially, as men whose dominant
interest was in questions of conduct, in clearing the field
of moral knowledge from the intrusion of duteous obli-
gations other than, or additional to, those concerning
which our own reason and conscience sufficiently inform
us.

Something of an intermediate position, which we shall
find reappearing in the work of later thinkers, is represented by the philosopher Spinoza. Reason has for him
undisputed right over the whole field of truth. Revelation,
on the other hand, is concerned only with obedience and

piety. The latter does indeed announce certain doctrines, but these, besides being of the simplest, are offered not so much because they are true as because they are conducive to obedience. Moreover, the obedience they demand coincides exactly with the moral requirements of the unaided reason and adds nothing to them. Yet revelation does perform one most necessary and valuable service—it assures us that the common man as well as the philosopher can achieve blessedness. In his own *Ethica* Spinoza will show that blessedness consists in the intellectual love of God, and that this love cannot arise out of simple faith but only out of rational philosophy.[3] But already, in the *Tractatus theologico-politicus,* he prepares the way for this somewhat melancholy conclusion by willingly allowing that, though "the power of reason does not extend so far as to determine for us that men may be blessed through simple obedience without understanding," revelation *does* tell us this, and indeed "tells us nothing else, . . . defining the dogmas of faith only in so far as they may be necessary for obedience, and leaving reason to determine their precise truth."[4] There is no need to question Spinoza's sincerity in saying this, or his satisfaction in being able to believe that, though he himself could find freedom and blessedness only at the end of an adventure of philosophic speculation, the simpler folk about him in his Dutch retreat could find something of both in their own way through obedience to the Biblical revelation.

So much for the rationalists; but among the early leaders

---

[3] *Ethica,* V, prop. 28. Conatus seu cupiditas cognoscendi res tertio cognitionis genere, oriri non potest ex primo; at quidem ex secundo cognitionis genere.

[4] *Tractatus theologico-politicus,* chap. xv.

of the Protestant Reformation the medieval balance of
reason and revelation had already been disturbed in a
very different and indeed opposite way. No more than the
rationalists did the Reformers quarrel with the terms of
the distinction but, taking a darker view than the medi-
evals of the corruption of human nature, they maintained
that human reason was now so damaged an instrument as
to yield little or no reliable knowledge of things divine.
Accordingly they touch but lightly upon natural theology
and base their systems almost wholly upon the revealed
Word. Luther, as is well known, has some particularly
hard things to say in contempt of reason, and also in contempt of the Scholastic theologians who made so much of
it; but at the same time this very turning aside from the
light of nature enabled him on occasion to conceive of
revelation in other terms than by means of its contrast
to that light, and thus to sow certain seeds of thought
which were to bear fruit in a much later period. Calvin, on
the other hand, begins his great *Institutes* by insisting that
there is a *sensus divinitatis* implanted in every human
mind and that the contemplation of the world of nature
furnishes us with further innumerable proofs—"not only
those more recondite which are contributed by astronomy,
medicine and physical science generally, but also such as
force themselves on the notice of the most uneducated of
men, who cannot open their eyes without having evidence
of them." [5] But he at once goes on to say that our sinful
dulness and blindness are such that we derive no profit
from these manifestations, so that as far as we are concerned they have been given in vain. Hence "God pre-
sents us with a matchless gift when He uses not dumb
teachers merely, for the instruction of the Church, but

[5] *Institutes of the Christian Religion*, I, chap. v, 2.

opens also His own holy mouth." [6] However, within the Protestant orthodoxy which was so soon to follow on the freer spirit of the first Reformers the light of reason was allowed considerably ampler room. Albrecht Ritschl complains that even Melanchthon, in the second edition of his *Loci,* already reverts to the practice of building "Christian doctrine on a foundation of natural theology after the Scholastic model, . . . thus abandoning Luther's principle." [7] Indeed he protests that Calvin himself, in beginning his *Institutes* with a discussion of natural religion and proceeding from that to the consideration of the Christian revelation, betrays a certain lapse from Luther's principle into something more like the old Scholasticism.[8] How much more must Ritschl have regretted the procedure of such later Calvinistic treatises as that from which quotation was made above!

Well before Ritschl's time, however, the prestige of natural theology had suffered serious diminution under pressure coming from another, though by no means wholly independent, quarter. Towards the end of the eighteenth century the reign of rationalist theology was challenged by the theological thought associated with the beginnings of the Romantic movement, and above all by the criticism of Immanuel Kant. It is difficult to think of Kant himself as a romantic, but he was influenced by Rousseau as well as reacting against him; and if he recoiled from Rousseau's sentimentalism, he recoiled even more strongly from the rationalist theology of the Leibnitzo-Wolffian school which had so largely affected him in his student days. The theo-

[6] *Ibid.,* chap. vi, 1.

[7] Ritschl, *Die Christliche Lehre von der Rechtfertigung und Versöhnung dargestellt* (3. Auflage; Bonn, 1889–1900), III, 7.

[8] Ritschl, *Theologie und Metaphysik* (2. Auflage; Bonn, 1887), p. 64.

retical exercise of reason, he contends, cannot conduct us
to any such knowledge of super-sensible reality as religion
requires. "I must therefore," he writes, "abolish knowledge
to make room for faith" [9]—which faith is religion's only
proper base. Here as elsewhere in his thought there is
undoubtedly traceable the influence of the Pietist movement under whose auspices he had been brought up in
both home and school. But Pietism, besides desiring to
abolish from Lutheran worship certain features of medieval practice which Luther had retained, had stood no
less for a recovery of those aspects of Luther's thought
which had been overlaid by later Lutheran dogmatism.
The Kantian rejection of natural theology is thus not
unconnected with Luther's earlier suppression of it. On
the other hand, the "faith" in whose interest Kant re-
jected it is very different from anything that Luther would
have recognized under that name. Though set in contrast with the exercise of the theoretical reason which
had issued in natural theology, it was still a rational faith
(*Vernunftglaube*), being in fact an exercise of what he
called—in a way that would have pleased Spinoza—the
practical reason. And when, on the completion of his great
critical trilogy, he was able to devote a whole volume
to the theological question, he entitled it *Religion inner-
halb der Grenzen der blossen Vernunft* (Religion within
the Limits of Reason Alone).

REVELATION IN THE CONTINENTAL PROTESTANTISM OF THE
NINETEENTH CENTURY

These influences, acting conjointly, were enough to ensure that the old natural theology, whether as practised

[9] Kant, *Kritik der reinen Vernunft,* Preface to 2d ed.

in the Middle Ages or by the rationalist thinkers of the succeeding centuries, should be little heard of among the leading Continental theologians of the nineteenth century outside the Roman communion. Furthermore, the tide of the Romantic movement set in with redoubled vigour in the period immediately following Kant's death in 1804, and among other things this ensured that many who followed him in preferring faith to speculative reason would resile from that remnant of rationalist thought in his system which made him still conceive of faith as an exercise of reason, though of another sort of reason.

Now it might be expected that when the old natural theology was thus out of use, and its "light of reason and nature" so sadly dimmed, we should all the time be hearing of revelation, and of revelation alone. Had the only influence leading to the change been that deriving from the teaching of the Reformers, we should certainly be doing so. In fact, however, the situation turned out very differently. A conception of revelation which had always defined it as providing a supplement to the findings of natural theology could hardly be left standing when natural theology was declared, as by Kant, to have no findings. Kant himself made no use of any concept of revelation. The faith which he laboured to defend was very far from being the acceptance of an authoritatively communicated truth, and this was the only meaning of the word with which tradition supplied him. The same is true not only of Hegel, but hardly less of the thinker who was so often spoken of, in the Continental Protestantism of the nineteenth century, as "the father of modern theology," namely Friedrich Schleiermacher. In his great system of doctrine, *Der christliche Glaube,* Schleiermacher's discussion of the conception of revelation is virtually confined to a single "postscript" in which he strives (and with very little success) to find a meaning for the word which he can reasonably fit into the rest of his thinking; [10] and in particular he reacts strongly against the idea of a revelation which "operates upon man as a cognitive being," and is therefore "originally and essentially *doctrine*." [11]

Schleiermacher's thought, like Kant's, had its Pietistic roots, but at the same time was caught into the stream of the Romantic movement to a degree that Kant's never was. These were not, however, entirely separate influences. Pietism, though itself a much older phenomenon, was undoubtedly one of the sources of German romanticism; just as the corresponding evangelical movement in England had its own contribution to make towards the emergence of the romantic temper in that country. What gave Schleiermacher the title of "father of modern theology" was that, steering his course between Protestant dogmatism on the one hand and philosophic rationalism on the other, he departed altogether from the old dichotomy of reason and revelation and found what seemed to be a middle way between the two. His theology rests neither on authoritatively communicated truths nor on truths excogitated by the speculative reason but on what he calls the religious self-consciousness of the Christian community. This self-consciousness is essentially a sense of complete dependence on God—and, in contradistinction from

[10] Schleiermacher, *Der christliche Glaube nach den Grundsätzen der evangelischen Kirche* (1921–22), §10.3, postscript. *Vide* pp. 47ff. of the English translation, *The Christian Faith,* ed. by H. R. Mackintosh and J. S. Stewart (Edinburgh, 1928).

[11] *Ibid.,* p. 50.

that of other religious communities, of dependence upon the redemption wrought by God in Christ. Romantic that he was, Schleiermacher conceived this consciousness of dependence not as a kind of cognition, but as a variety of feeling. In this he found few to follow him; but his more general contention that theology takes its rise in the religious consciousness, and that all its doctrines are but explications of this consciousness, became the foundation of much Protestant thought throughout the nineteenth century.

The same dissatisfaction with the old dichotomy, and the desire to find a ground for faith which should be neither the acceptance of authoritatively communicated truths on the one hand nor the speculations of the old natural theology on the other, appear independently in several of Schleiermacher's contemporaries, both older and younger. Lessing and Jacobi had already moved far in that direction, but most important of all is Hegel, who was Schleiermacher's colleague and rival in the University of Berlin between 1818 and 1831. To him, as to Schleiermacher, all piety rests on the immediate utterances of the religious consciousness, and all Christian piety on those of the Christian consciousness; but such consciousness characteristically grasps truth in the form of images (*Vorstellungen*), and it is the office of rational philosophy to translate these images into concepts (*Begriffe*), purging them of their merely imaginative and symbolic character and so conducting us to an exacter form of knowledge. To Hegel, therefore, the content of Christian faith and that of his own philosophy are one and the same. The former is, as it were, a first apprehension of the latter; an apprehension adequate enough as the foundation of piety,

though inadequate as conceptual knowledge. Here again
we are reminded of Spinoza.

As the nineteenth century proceeded, there was heated
debate in Germany between the theologians who followed
this lead of Hegel's and those who stood rather in the suc-
cession of Schleiermacher. Much the most influential of
the latter was Ritschl, himself the historian of Pietism,
and it was his school which ultimately secured for itself
by far the largest following. In his view all theological
knowledge rests upon what he calls "the value-judgments
of faith"; nor should we

strive after a purely theoretical or "disinterested" knowledge
of God as an indispensable preliminary to the knowledge of
faith. To be sure, people say that we must first know the
nature of God and Christ ere we can ascertain their value for
us. But Luther's insight perceived the incorrectness of such
a view. The truth rather is that we know the nature of God
and Christ only *in* their value for us.[12]

Ritschl has thus no place in his thought for a rational
knowledge of God that is precedent to faith. But neither
has he place for a revelation conceived as the authoritative
communication of doctrine. His theology, like that of the
others of whom we have spoken, has not a double but
a single source; and that single source corresponds to
neither term of the old dichotomy but is in a sense intermediate between them, perhaps partaking in some degree of the character of each. Ritschl himself still makes
use of the concept of revelation, though in a changed

[12] Ritschl, *Rechtfertigung und Versöhnung,* III, §29. The above is
slightly amended from the English translation by H. R. Mackintosh and
A. B. Macaulay, *The Christian Doctrine of Justification and Reconcilia-
tion; The Positive Development of the Doctrine* (Edinburgh and New
York, 1900).

sense; but there is no doubt that in many quarters, and as a result of the same general development, it suffered virtual suppression. I shall be contending that this represented a loss of the most serious kind, yet it is not difficult to see the reason for it. It is as if these thinkers felt revelation to be so universally understood as the verbal or conceptual communication of truth by divine authority that only by abandoning the term itself could they effectively retreat from this wrong meaning.

REVELATION IN NINETEENTH-CENTURY BRITAIN

Finally we may ask how far this development within continental Protestantism influenced the thought of nineteenth-century Britain. The picture here presented is more complex. In certain circles the Oxford Movement brought with it a renewed adherence to the medieval pattern, and, as has been well said:

For Scholasticism, whether in its original form or as modified by teachers of our own time, the concept of revelation as the supernatural and infallible communication of propositional truths is indispensable. . . . Thomism lays a broad foundation of natural theology, but its most distinctive feature is the clear line which it draws between the two.[13]

Moreover, quite apart from that or any other new movement, the conservative forces within Protestantism retained a firmer hold on Britain than on the Continent, and this ensured among other things that natural theology of the old type should continue to be accorded an honourable place. To mention only one example, in 1836 the eminent Scottish evangelical divine, Thomas Chalmers, published

[13] Creed, *The Divinity of Jesus Christ*, p. 114.

the two volumes of his *Natural Theology* in which he followed very much the traditional line, protesting against the "confused imagination" harboured by some timid spirits that "every new accession, whether of evidence or of doctrine, made to the Natural, tends in so far to reduce the claims or to depreciate the importance of the Christian Theology." [14]

On the other hand (and beginning perhaps with Coleridge) both Kant and Schleiermacher, and afterwards Ritschl, made their influence felt in many quarters, if somewhat belatedly. There was accordingly a wide area of English and Scottish theological thought in which the old disjunction of natural and revealed knowledge played little part, sometimes no part at all. A distinction which had once appeared so clear and easy to understand was one to which it now seemed difficult to assign any unambiguous meaning. The concept of revelation was variously submitted to critical analysis, but often in a way that appeared to abate its former high significance; and there were some who gave it no real place in their thought.[15] By his bequest of 1887 Lord Gifford founded in the four Scottish universities the well-known lectureships which bear his name, with a view to the promotion and diffusion of natural theology, "treated as a strictly natural science like astronomy or chemistry, without reference to or reliance upon any supposed special, exceptional or so-called miraculous revelation"; but not a few

[14] Thomas Chalmers, "On Natural Theology," *The Works of Thomas Chalmers, D.D.* (Glasgow, London, 1836–49), II, 414.

[15] "In the nineteenth century it becomes less usual than it had been to speak of Christianity as 'Revealed Religion,' and commoner to speak of it as 'a historical religion' or 'the Historic Faith.'" Creed, *The Divinity of Jesus Christ*, p. 104.

of the lecturers were to find themselves embarrassed by this renewed insistence upon the terms of the old distinction. Lecturing on the foundation in 1890–91, the eminent Scottish preacher and vice-chancellor, John Caird, who knew his Schleiermacher as well as his beloved Hegel, protested against the distinction between natural and revealed religion as an "arbitrary" and "misleading" one "which has come down to us as a legacy from the rationalistic theologians of last [i.e. of the eighteenth] century." [16] He contended that

Revealed truth cannot belong to a different order from all other truth that appeals to the human consciousness. . . . On the contrary, by universal admission the teaching of revelation finds its best and only sufficient evidence in the consciousness of the believer.[17]

At the same time there is no such thing as a natural religion which is independent of all revelation. As he had already argued in an earlier work,

Neither thought nor the aspirations of the religious nature can be satisfied with the rationalistic notion of a merely subjective religion—of opinions and beliefs wrought out by the spontaneous activity of the human mind, and involving nothing more on the divine side than is involved in the original creation of man's rational nature.[18]

Thus "the primary organ of religious knowledge is not reason but faith." [19] This faith, however, is for him, as for

[16] John Caird, *The Fundamental Ideas of Christianity* (Glasgow, 1899), I, 4, 13, 16.

[17] *Ibid.*, pp. 16f.

[18] John Caird, *An Introduction to the Philosophy of Religion* (Glasgow, 1880), p. 60.

[19] Caird, *Fundamental Ideas of Christianity*, p. 39.

his master Hegel, nothing but "implicit reason, reason working intuitively and unconsciously, without reflection or criticism of its own operations"; [20] and the fact that we must begin with it "is no reason why we should not go on to mediated or scientific knowledge." [21]

It is thus very evident that during the course of the nineteenth century the time-honoured conception of revelation, which defined it in terms of an absolute distinction between the deliverances of the unaided intellect and the acceptance of divinely communicated information, had lost its meaning for many of the leading thinkers. The traditional procedure had—to put it in its baldest form— been first to set down such truths about God as could be reached by rational speculation, and then to advance to those supplementary truths for which we must be dependent on revelation alone. The contribution of revelation thus tended to be conceived in terms of comparison and contrast with its non-revelational preamble, to which it was regarded as essentially forming a supplement. What it had to offer us, when we had come to the end of our own researches, was not something of an entirely different order, but *more of the same,* though deriving from an entirely different source. We cannot regret that such a conception should have been departed from; while on the other hand we cannot be too thankful that in our own century, though not without the aid of foreshadowings in earlier periods, a new and better understanding of the meaning of revelation is beginning to emerge.

[20] *Ibid.,* p. 46.   [21] *Ibid.,* p. 39.

II: The Divine Self-Disclosure

Revelation literally means an unveiling, the lifting of an obscuring veil, so as to disclose something that was formerly hidden. To disclose means to uncover, but in ordinary usage it does not mean to discover. I discover something for myself, but I disclose it to another. Or I say of one thing that I have discovered it, but of another that it has been disclosed to me; in the former case thinking of myself as primarily active, but in the latter as primarily passive.

There is a sense in which all valid knowledge, all apprehended truth may be regarded as revealed. Knowledge is indeed an activity of the human mind, yet not a creative activity but only a responsive one. There can be no valid knowledge except of what is already there, either waiting or striving to be known. The knowing mind is active in attending, selecting, and interpreting; but it must attend to, select from, and interpret what is presented to it; and therefore it must be passive as well as active. Here is a passage from a philosopher who, in his attempt to analyse

the nature of even the most ordinary knowledge, finds it
necessary to have recourse to the vocabulary of revelation:

When we perceive, no doubt we are active—we attend, select,
engage our interest. But what we perceive comes to us; it is
not mainly, and originally never, of our choosing, still less of
our making. . . . So again in thinking we are active, but
what we think, once more, comes to us: the object of thought
reveals itself to us, it determines our thinking. Wherever our
thinking is good thinking, it is under control of the object.
When we are logically compelled to think so and not otherwise, then what we think is true. When we reflect on these
familiar facts, the "activity" of the mind begins to wear a
different face. It threatens almost to pass into passivity. . . . In
most ways it would be truer to say that "our" activity (the
activity of "our" minds) is the activity of *what*, as object or
content, fills our minds. If "I think" is one side of the truth,
certainly "the world thinks in me" or "reveals itself in my
thinking" is the other side.[1]

These words are all the more significant as coming from
an idealist philosopher, because idealists are suspected of
regarding the object as a sort of emanation of the subject, but what is here affirmed is that all true knowledge is
knowledge which is determined not by the subject but
by the object. Here is how another philosopher puts it:

The highest achievement of Reason is attained when the
mind is so completely informed by its object that there is as
little as possible in the notion we have of the object which
belongs to our way of apprehending it, and not really to the
object itself.[2]

With this we must certainly agree. I see or hear aright
when my seeing or hearing is determined, in every par-

[1] R. F. Alfred Hoernlé, *Idealism as a Philosophy* (London and New
York, 1927), pp. 71ff.
[2] Webb, *Problems in the Relations of God and Man*, p. 45.

ticular, by what is there to be seen or heard. The right answer to an arithmetical problem is the one which is wholly determined by the figures facing me. I think validly when my thought is completely controlled by the facts before me. If it be said that I manipulate these facts by means of the laws of thought, it must be answered that these laws of thought are not laws of mind in the sense that so-called natural laws are laws of nature. They do not tell us how the mind operates, but how it ought to operate. They are, therefore, laws *for* thought rather than *of* thought, laws to which mind is obliged to conform if it is to attain true knowledge. And the reason why mind is thus obliged to conform to them is that they are laws of the reality which mind is attempting to know. They are not descriptive of mind but only normative for it; what they are descriptive of is the most general relations subsisting between the objects with which mind is confronted. Here we may quote a third philosopher—one belonging this time to the realist school:

Philosophers have commonly held that the laws of logic, which underlie mathematics, are laws of thought, laws regulating the operation of our minds. By this opinion the true dignity of reason is very greatly lowered; it ceases to be an investigation into the very heart and immutable essence of all things actual and possible, becoming, instead, an enquiry into something more or less human and subject to our limitations. . . . It is only when we thoroughly understand the entire independence of ourselves which belongs to this world that reason finds, that we can adequately realise the profound importance of its beauty.[3]

It is important to make this point because many theologians, in their anxiety to establish or conserve a clear

[3] Bertrand Russell, *Mysticism and Logic* (London, 1918), pp. 68f.

distinction between divine revelation and what they have called rational knowledge, have made this task much too easy for themselves by speaking as if, while the former is something given to us, the latter is something we create for ourselves, as it were spun out of our own substance; as if the former must be explained by beginning from the realities apprehended, whereas the latter could be explained by beginning from the apprehending mind. They have thus, in the language of our last quotation, been guilty of an illicit lowering of the dignity of reason in order to exalt the dignity of revelation; and no good can come of such procedure. The fact is that no true knowledge, no valid act of perceiving or thinking, can be explained by beginning from the human end—whether it be my perception of the number of peas in a particular pod or my discovery of an argument for the existence of God. In either case my cognition is valid only so far as it is determined by the reality with which I am faced. In the latter case, of course, the reality facing me need not, so far as our present point is concerned, be God Himself. It may consist only of facts coercively pointing to Him; just as the reality directly confronting Adams and Leverrier, when they validly inferred the existence of Neptune, was not the planet itself but certain other phenomena which coercively pointed to its existence.

Thus we can understand why the philosopher whom we began by quoting should speak of all knowledge, in its distinction from false opinion, as being revealed. But is then the revelation of which the Bible speaks only a special case of this? Does it mean only that, like the rest of objective reality, God is there, independently of us, waiting to be known, so that our knowledge of Him is true and valid in proportion as we allow it to be controlled by what, on investigation, we actually find Him to be? A well-known poem of Wordsworth perhaps suggests such an answer:

> The eye—it cannot choose but see;
> We cannot bid the ear be still;
> Our bodies feel, where'er they be,
> Against or with our will.
>
> Nor less I deem that there are Powers
> Which of themselves our minds impress;
> That we can feed this mind of ours
> In a wise passiveness.
>
> Think you, 'mid all this mighty sum
> Of things for ever speaking,
> That nothing of itself will come,
> But we must still be seeking? [4]

That may be taken to mean that, whereas a too active and questing frame of mind may defeat its own purpose, so that what is required is rather a certain passive waiting for the Powers themselves to impress us, yet in their turn these Powers (whatever they are!) are merely waiting to be known by us, and not necessarily taking any initiative of an active kind to ensure that we do not remain ignorant of them. That would accord with Wordsworth's general conception of the "presence that disturbs me with the joy of elevated thoughts" and the "something"

> Whose dwelling is the light of setting suns,
> And the round ocean and the living air,
> And the blue sky, and in the mind of man:

[4] *Expostulation and Reply* (1798).

> A motion and a spirit, that impels
> All thinking things, all objects of all thought,
> And rolls through all things.[5]

It looks as if Wordsworth does not conceive of this "presence," this "something," this "spirit," as a Being who, besides being known by him, also has knowledge of Wordsworth and therefore seeks to be known by Wordsworth. Or at least such a conception would be otiose, since he ascribes to the "presence" no behaviour which necessitates it. In other words, he does not think of the "presence" as One with whom he can have personal relations. Had he done so, he must have written quite otherwise. He would then, in fact, have written much more as do the Biblical authors. For the revelation of which the Bible speaks is always such as has place within a personal relationship. It is not the revelation of an object to a subject, but a revelation from subject to subject, a revelation of mind to mind. That is the first thing that differentiates the theological meaning of revelation, the revelation that is made to faith, from the sense in which all valid knowledge has been said to be revelation.

The theological usage is therefore not a special case of this general epistemological usage. Rather is it the other way about. The theological usage of the term is the primary one, and the other is weakened from this and is, in fact, only a metaphor. We have acknowledged the complete justification of the point the epistemologists were desirous of making, yet we cannot accept the phrase "The object of thought reveals itself to me" as anything but metaphorical. The object of thought itself undertakes no unveiling. When we thus speak of it we are personifying

[5] *Lines, composed a few miles above Tintern Abbey* (1798).

it; and this fact justifies the statement that, properly speaking, revelation has place only within the relationship of person to person.

But now a further qualification is necessary. Having differentiated the revelation of mind to mind from the revelation of object to mind, we must now further differentiate the revelation of divine to human mind from the revelation of one human mind to another. The former is much more deeply mysterious, but indeed the latter is mysterious enough. It defies precise analysis. I cannot possibly analyse for you, in any exhaustive way, how my friend revealed himself to me as what he is. Sometimes a man whom I have never met before reveals much of himself to me during a casual meeting of a few minutes; he "gives himself away," as we say. Sometimes we even think we know something about a man at a first glance. But we find it exceedingly difficult to say *how* we know. Our reflective analysis may carry us some way towards an explanation, but never all the way, or nearly all the way.

Moreover, this difficulty attaches not only to our way of knowing, but also to the content of the knowledge. When I try to tell you what I have found my friend to be, when I try to describe to you his personality or mind or character, it is impossible that I should do this exhaustively. My description will take the form either of cataloguing some of the qualities I have found in him, or of recounting a few revealing words or actions of his, or most probably it will be a combination of both. But no part of this description can be exhaustive. If I recount some of his words and actions, and choose my examples well, it may be that by means of them you will succeed in grasping something of the man himself; but that is only because you fill up what is lacking out of your own knowledge of other personalities to which you think my friend's personality must be in some degree analogous. And when I recount my friend's qualities, what I am doing is trying to fix certain aspects of my friend's personality in a number of abstract nouns. In other words I am *abstracting* something from the living tissue of his personality. But no number of such abstractions can exhaust the fullness of a living personality. Abstract nouns

> half reveal,
> And half conceal, the soul within.

That is, each abstract noun I apply gives you a partly wrong impression of the man at the same time as it conducts you towards a right impression. I can correct this by making one abstraction modify another, as when I say that he is "brave without being foolhardy," or "humble without being cringing," but in all this I am but narrowing the type to which he belongs, rather than offering you the individual.

All these considerations apply with greatly increased force to the revelation of God to the human soul. It is doubly impossible that we should give exhaustive account either of the ways by which we know God or of the God whom we know. For God is not, like my friend, merely one being among others, but is the source of all being. While therefore my friend's relations with me can only be through the very limited medium of his own psycho-somatic organisation, there is nothing through which God cannot reveal Himself to me.[6]

Moreover, as to the God who is revealed, theology at-

6 See below, p. 74ff.

tempts to give an account of Him, a *logos* of *theos,* by an enumeration of "attributes" which are all expressed in abstract nouns. Yet no such enumeration of His attributes can be more than rough and ready; and none can be complete. In the deed of foundation of a well-known lectureship at Cambridge, each lecturer is instructed to deal with one or more of the attributes of God, but "when these are exhausted," he may go on to some other subject. But they can never be exhausted. The infinite riches of the divine Personality who is revealed to us in Christ cannot be exhaustively enclosed in any number of abstract nouns. In every such abstraction, in every such conceptualizing, we are also to some extent falsifying by regarding one aspect of a living whole in temporary isolation; and not all possible abstractions added together can make up the living whole itself.

DISCLOSURE OF SUBJECT TO SUBJECT

All revelation, then, is from subject to subject, and the revelation with which we are here concerned is from the divine Subject to the human. But there is a further distinction that must be drawn. We speak, as has been said, of a man's revealing himself, that is, his character and mind and will, to his fellow, but we also sometimes speak of a man's revealing to his fellow certain items of knowledge other than knowledge of himself. I may say, for instance, that a friend has "revealed" to me the proof of a geometrical theorem, the best way of roasting a partridge, or the number of apple trees in his orchard. This is, however, to use the term in a very much weakened sense, such as in many languages would appear a little precious. The Greek ἀποκαλύπτειν, the Latin *revelare,* the German *offenbaren,* are words too exalted to be used naturally in this way. Only if the information offered were something of a secret, as for instance the location of a rare wild flower, would such a word sometimes be called into service; or still more if what was in question was the "unveiling" of some "mystery."

In the Bible the word is always used in its proper and exalted sense. Not only is revelation always "the revelation of a mystery which was kept secret for long ages but is now disclosed," [7] but the mystery thus disclosed is nothing less than God's own will and purpose. According to the Bible, what is revealed to us is not a body of information concerning various things of which we might otherwise be ignorant. If it is information at all, it is information concerning the nature and mind and purpose of God—that and nothing else. Yet in the last resort it is not information about God that is revealed, but very God Himself incarnate in Jesus Christ our Lord. If we consult Kittel's *Theological Dictionary of the New Testament,* which is as nearly impartial and as little tendentious a work of scholarship as is available, we shall be told that in the Old Testament

revelation is *not* the communication of supranatural knowledge, and *not* the stimulation of numinous feelings. The revelation can indeed give rise to knowledge and is necessarily accompanied by numinous feelings; yet it does not itself consist in these things but is quite essentially the *action* of Yahweh, an unveiling of His essential hiddenness, His offering of Himself in fellowship.

While in the New Testament,

revelation is likewise understood, not in the sense of a communication of supranatural knowledge, but in the sense of a self-disclosure of God.[8]

[7] Rom. 16. 25f.

[8] *S.v.* καλύπτω, pp. 575, 586. The article is by Professor Albrecht Oepke of Leipzig.

The recovery of this fundamental insight is the first thing we notice as running broadly throughout all the recent discussions, marking them off from the formulations of earlier periods. From a very early time in the history of the Church the tendency had manifested itself to equate divine revelation with a body of information which God has communicated to man, this information being in part about God Himself, but including also very much that could not be thus described, even to such historical facts as the dates of accession of the kings of Israel and Judah, and the genealogy of Joseph the husband of Mary. Behind this tendency lay a strong sense of the necessity of preserving unity of doctrine throughout the Church—in other words, a growing sense of the necessity of ὄρθη δόξα, right opinion, orthodoxy. A beginning of it can already be detected in the latest books of the New Testament itself, but it appears much more plainly in the generation following, and then grows apace. Its natural culmination was in the simple identification of revelation with the total content of Holy Scripture. A lead had already been given in this direction by the insistence of the Rabbis within later Judaism that the Old Testament law and prophets represented the *ipsissima verba* of God; and now the same principle was extended to the Gospels and the Epistles. It was carried to a greater extreme in the West than in the East, until finally the Roman Church, at the Council of Trent, defined that the whole of Scripture, as well as a body of unwritten tradition, had been given *Spiritu sancto dictante,* at the dictation of the Holy Spirit.[9] In the Catechism prepared by the same Council we are told that

whereas the things divinely revealed are so many and so various that it is no easy task either to acquire a knowledge of

[9] *Sessio quarta, Decretum de canonicis Scripturis.*

them or, having acquired such knowledge, to retain them in the memory, . . . our ancestors have wisely reduced the whole force and system of the doctrine of faith to these four heads: the Apostles' Creed, the Sacraments, the Ten Commandments, and the Lord's Prayer; . . .[10]

which four heads then form the four divisions of the Catechism. How far we have travelled from the New Testament when we think of God's revelation as being of such a kind as to put a strain on the memory! It is significant also that the section of the Catechism from which the above is quoted bears the caption, "Since God hath withdrawn His visible presence from us, His pastors derive His Word from Scripture and from Tradition." Surely there is something seriously wrong in this way of putting it—in saying that God has so withdrawn Himself as to leave us with only a script and a memory!

Yet such a statement follows the teaching of St. Thomas Aquinas and his fellow Dominicans faithfully enough, though both the Franciscan theologians and the earlier Augustinians would have been uncomfortable with it. Moreover, even those modern theologians outside the Roman Church who veer in a Thomist direction will often be found speaking in much the same way. In his very able Bampton Lectures, to which we shall presently be referring at greater length, Dr. Austin Farrer criticises in the following terms the view that "God is not to be known by us unless He reveals Himself *personally*":

What does it mean? On the face of it, it suggests that God must speak to us somewhat as we speak to one another. But this obviously does not happen, nor is it going to happen. . . .

[10] Preface to the Catechism, *Quaestio* xii.

Neither out of the Scripture I read nor in the prayers I tried to make did any mental voice address me. . . . And this is why, when Germans set their eye-balls and pronounce the terrific words "He speaks to thee" (*Er redet dich an*), I am sure indeed that they are saying something, but I am still more sure that they are not speaking to my condition.[11]

The Vatican Council of 1869–70 repeated the Tridentine phrase "At the dictation of the Holy Spirit"; and in 1893 Leo XIII repeated it again in his encyclical *Providentissimus Deus:*

All the books and the whole of each book which the Church receives as sacred and canonical were written at the dictation of the Holy Spirit; and so far is it from being possible that any error can co-exist with divine inspiration that not only does the latter in itself exclude all error, but excludes and rejects it with the same necessity as attaches to the impossibility that God Himself, who is the supreme Truth, should be the author of any error whatever.[12]

This simple identification of divine revelation with Holy Scripture was carried forward into the churches of the Reformation, becoming no less characteristic of Protestantism than of the Counter-Reformation. Something different might have been expected. The Reformers professed to stand for a return to a more Biblical understanding of faith; and since faith is the correlate of revelation, being the disposition of mind in which revelation is received, nothing would have been more natural than a simultaneous return to a view of revelation more like the Biblical one.

[11] Farrer, *The Glass of Vision* (Westminster [London], 1948), p. 8.
[12] *Vide* H. J. D. Denzinger and Clemens Bannwart, *Enchiridion symbolorum definitionum et declarationum de rebus fidei et morum* (21st ed., 1937), p. 544.

In Luther himself such a movement is very plainly discernible, but hardly at all in the thought of his successors. Dr. Emil Brunner writes that

The difference that exists among the theologians of the Reformation in regard to their attitude towards Scripture is not so much one of confession as one of generation. The Reformers of the first generation, Luther and Zwingli, are not favourable to the doctrine of verbal inspiration, while Melanchthon, Calvin and Bullinger are. Calvin is fond of speaking of the *oracula Dei,* and is very happy with the concept of divine dictation. Such critical pronouncements as Luther made about the writings of the Old and New Testaments are unthinkable in him, however much he recognizes the human side of Scripture when he comes to exegesis.[13]

Dr. Karl Barth similarly complains that the theologians of the immediately succeeding period—what he calls *der spätere Altprotestantismus*—made of Holy Scripture "a static sum of revealed propositions to be formed into a system like the paragraphs of a legal document," [14] so that "In all the utterances of this transition period we are painfully conscious of the loss of the Reformers' insight. . . . This shows itself in the doctrine of inspiration, which signifies what may be called a freezing up of the connection between Scripture and revelation." [15]

TRUTHS AND IMAGES

The present wide acceptance in this country of the view that revelation is not merely *from* Subject to subject, but also *of* Subject to subject, and that what God reveals to us

[13] Brunner, *Offenbarung und Vernunft, die Lehre von der christlichen Glaubenserkenntnis,* p. 126n.
[14] Barth, *Die kirchliche Dogmatik,* 1. Bd., p. 142.
[15] *Ibid.,* p. 127.

is Himself and not merely a body of propositions about Himself, owes much to the teaching of Archbishop William Temple, though his biographer tells us that Dr. Temple himself acknowledged his own great debt in this matter to Father Herbert Kelly.[16] Passages like the following have been very widely quoted:

What is offered to man's apprehension in any specific revelation is not truth concerning God but the living God Himself.[17]

There is no such thing as revealed truth. There are truths of revelation; but they are not themselves directly revealed.[18]

Under the influence of that exaggerated intellectualism which Christian Theology inherited from Greek Philosophy, a theory of revelation has usually been accepted in the Christian Church which fits very ill with the actual revelation treasured by the Church, . . . that through revelation we receive divinely guaranteed Truths.[19]

The same point had, however, been as clearly made by Wilhelm Herrmann of Marburg as early as 1887:

The thoughts contained in Scripture are not themselves the content of revelation. . . . On the contrary, we must already be renewed and redeemed by revelation before we can enter into the thought-world of Scripture. What then is the content of revelation, if it is not the doctrines of Scripture? There should surely be no doubt among Christians about the answer. One must have practised much unfruitful theology and been subjected to much bad teaching if one hesitates at all. For the Christian, and indeed for devout men everywhere, who seek God alone, it goes without saying that *God* is the

---

[16] F. A. Iremonger, *William Temple, Archbishop of Canterbury; his life and letters* (London, New York; 1948), pp. 532f.

[17] Temple, *Nature, Man and God*, p. 322.   [18] *Ibid.*, p. 316.

[19] Baillie and Martin, eds., *Revelation*, p. 101.

content of revelation. *All revelation* is the self-revelation of God.[20]

What this means is clear. The truths which Christians believe, the doctrines and dogmas which their Church teaches, are such as they could not be in possession of, if God had not first revealed Himself to His people—revealed His nature and mind and will and the purpose which, conformable to His will, He has in mind for their salvation. The propositions which the Bible contains, and likewise the propositions contained in the Church's creeds and dogmatic definitions and theological systems are all attempts, on however different levels, on the part of those who have received this revelation to express something of what it portends. They are far from being "unaided" attempts. The Biblical writers could not have written what they did, had the Holy Spirit of God not been with them and in them as they wrote. Nor could the later dogmatic labours of the Church have been carried through without ever-present divine assistance. Nevertheless the distinction must be kept clearly in mind between the divine and the human elements in the process, however inextricably these may be intermingled in the result. In what is given by God there can be no imperfection of any kind, but there is always imperfection in what we may be allowed to call the "receiving apparatus."

But let us now further hear Dr. Barth on this matter. Of the Bible he writes as follows:

Why and wherein does the Biblical witness possess authority? Precisely in this, that it claims no authority at all for itself, that its witness consists in allowing that Other Thing

[20] Herrmann, *Der Begriff der Offenbarung* (1887); reprinted in *Offenbarung und Wunder* (Giessen, 1908), pp. 9f.

to be itself and through itself the authority. Hence we do the
Bible a misdirected honour, and one unwelcome to itself, if
we directly identify it with this Other Thing, the revelation
itself. This can happen . . . in the form of a doctrine of the
general and uniform inspiration of the Bible.[21]

Revelation has to do with the Jesus Christ who was to come
and who finally, when the time was fulfilled, did come—
and so with the actual, literal Word spoken now really and
directly by God Himself. Whereas in the Bible we have to
do in all cases with human attempts to repeat and reproduce
this Word of God in human thoughts and words with reference to particular human situations, e.g. in regard to the com-
plications of the political position of Israel midway between
Egypt and Babylon, or to the errors and confusions of the
Christian congregation in Corinth between A.D. 50 and 60.
In the one case *Deus dixit,* but in the other *Paulus dixit;* and
these are two different things.[22]

Of the later dogmatic definitions of the Church Dr. Barth
writes further:

Dogmas are not *veritates a Deo formaliter revelatae.* In
dogmas it is the Church of the past that speaks—worthy of
honour, worthy of respect, normative, *non sine Deo,* as befits
her—but still the Church. She defines, that is she encloses in
dogmas, the revealed truth, the Word of God. And thereby
the Word of God becomes the word of man, not unworthy of
attention, but rather supremely worthy of attention, but still
the word of man.[23]

Is *veritas revelata* the truth of a doctrinal proposition? Is
the truth of revelation . . . . like other truths in that one can

---

[21] Barth, *Die kirchliche Dogmatik,* p. 115. Where I have translated as
"general and uniform," Barth has three adjectives, *"allegemeinen,
gleichmässigen und dauernden";* but I am not sure what the third of
these is intended to mean in this connection.

[22] *Ibid.,* p. 116.   [23] *Ibid.,* pp. 281f.

lay it down as ἀλήθεια, that is, as the result of the unveiling of a hidden character by means of human ideas, concepts and judgments, and as being, so to say, preserved in this confined and defined form, even apart from the event of its becoming unveiled? Can one possess it in abstraction from the Person of Him who reveals it and from the revelatory act of that Person—the act in which that Person gives Himself to be perceived by another person? If the truth of revelation is the truth of a doctrinal proposition, then obviously we must answer, Yes.[24]

From Dr. Temple and Dr. Barth let us turn now to Dr. Austin Farrer, and to his Bampton Lectures of which mention has already been made. Only with some reluctance does he agree that divine revelation is not given in the form of propositional truths:

In taking up the topic of Scriptural inspiration, we should like to attach ourselves to the thought of the ancient Church; but this, we are told, is just what we have not to do. For, it is said, pre-modern thought on the subject was vitiated by a single and cardinal false assumption—the assumption that revelation was given in the form of propositions. The sacred writers were supposed to have been moved by it matters not what process of mind to put down on paper a body of propositions which, as they stand on the paper, are *de facto* inerrant. It is now impossible, we are told, to get anywhere from here. We now recognize that the propositions on the Scriptural page express the response of human witnesses to divine events, not a miraculous divine dictation.[25]

Dr. Farrer, however, submits that this theory of revelation by divine events alone is no more satisfying than the theory of dictated propositions. That question will be before us

[24] *Ibid.,* p. 285.   [25] Farrer, *The Glass of Vision,* pp. 36f.

in a later chapter, but we must meanwhile consider the alternative view which Dr. Farrer himself offers. "This at least," he tells us, "in modern thought upon the subject is true: the primary revelation is Jesus Christ Himself." [26] But Christ's own thought was characteristically expressed in the form of *images*—such dominant images as the Kingdom of God, the Son of Man, the Israel of God, and "the infinitely complex and fertile image of sacrifice and communion, of expiation and covenant." And Dr. Farrer's generalized conclusion is that "divine truth is supernaturally communicated to men in an act of inspired thinking which falls into the shape of certain images." [27] More fully, he writes as follows:

These tremendous images, and others like them, are not the whole of Christ's teaching, but they set forth the supernatural mystery which is the heart of the teaching. Without them, the teaching would not be supernatural revelation, but instruction in piety and morals. It is because the spiritual instruction is related to the great images that it becomes revealed truth. . . .

The great images interpreted the events of Christ's ministry, death and resurrection, and the events interpreted the images; the interplay of the two is revelation. Certainly the events without the images would be no revelation at all, and the images without the events would remain shadows on the clouds. . . .

In the apostolic mind . . . the God-given images lived, not statically, but with an inexpressible creative force. . . . The stuff of inspiration is living images. . . .

We have to listen to the Spirit speaking divine things: and the way to appreciate his speech is to quicken our own minds with the life of inspired images. . . .

[26] *Ibid.*, p. 39.   [27] *Ibid.*, p. 57.

Theology tests and determines the sense of the images, it does not create it. The images, of themselves, signify and reveal.[28]

We cannot but be grateful to Dr. Farrer for the emphasis he has laid, both here and in his other writings, on the part played in divine revelation by the great archetypal images of our faith. There is no doubt that in what philosophers and theologians have written concerning the modes of religious apprehension far less than justice has been done to the office of the imagination as against the intellect. But the case which he here attempts to make rests upon an exaggeration of the distinctness, each from the other, of these two sides of our mental life. In the thought of St. Paul, for example, images and propositional truths are inextricably intermingled, and it is difficult to know why we should suppose that the former are directly the medium of revelation in a sense in which the latter are not. At least part of Dr. Farrer's reason for speaking thus of the images seems to be that he hopes the position he now adopts will turn the edge of the objection to the idea of plenary inspiration. What cannot be affirmed of propositional truths will, he hopes, be conceded to images. This, however, can be only if it is believed that, whereas all propositional apprehension of truth contains a human element and therefore an element of possible error, the images are given directly by God and contain no such element. But what possible ground have we for such a discrmination? The human imagination is in itself just as fallible as the judgement-forming intellect, and it is difficult to find a reason for believing that revelation exercises a more coercive control over the one than over the other.

[28] *Ibid.*, pp. 42–44.

Dr. Temple, it will be remembered, was quoted as saying that "what is offered to man's apprehension in any specific revelation is not truth concerning God, but the living God Himself." We should now be inclined to add, "And not images pointing to God, but the living God Himself." For the deepest difficulty felt about the equation of revelation with communicated truths is that it offers us something less than personal encounter and personal communion; and that difficulty is in no way relieved by the proposal to replace communicated truths by implanted images. We must not indeed forget Dr. Farrer's sufficiently emphatic statement that "the primary revelation is Jesus Christ Himself"; and we have his other statement that "the images themselves are not what is principally revealed: they are no more than the instruments by which realities are to be known." Yet to this is added at once the rider that "nothing but the image is given us to act as an indication of the reality. We cannot appeal from the images to the reality, for by hypothesis we have not got the reality, except in the form which the images signify." [29] This, as Dr. Farrer realises, at once suggests the question, "Does God feed his saints with nothing but figures of speech?" It is a question, he says, which "does not admit of a yes-or-no answer." Certainly we are given something of "a foretaste or earnest of supernatural life," without which indeed "revealed truth is dumb to us"; but on the other hand "there is no sort of proportion" between the foretaste and the truth we believe, such that the latter could be drawn out of the former alone.[30] Such a statement, however, carries conviction only by concealing an ambiguity. None of us could hold for a moment that such a participation in "supernat-

[29] *Ibid.*, pp. 57f.   [30] *Ibid.*, p. 59.

ural life" as has been granted to us is proportionate to the whole revelation received by the prophets and apostles. No claim of that kind can possibly be here in question. The only proportion we should be concerned to affirm is between such revelation as the prophets and apostles were enabled to receive and the measure of "supernatural life" which *they themselves* were enabled to enjoy. To say that God directly injected into their minds archetypal images or symbols which did not grow out of, and were not matched by, the living communion with God which had been granted to them, and by the love of God shed abroad in their hearts by the Holy Spirit which was given to them,[31] would be a reversion to that mechanical idea of inspiration which is absent from the prophetic and apostolic writings themselves and from which, though it has been common enough in later Christian thought, most of us are anxious to depart.

[31] Rom. 5. 5.

III: Aspects of the Revealed Content

OUR ULTIMATE CONCERN

In however varying forms and degrees, mankind has always had the sense that life portended something more than appeared upon its surface. On the surface it was busy enough and perhaps also interesting enough. Men have always had plenty to do and plenty to think about, plenty both to occupy their hands and to preoccupy their minds. Yet they have ever been convinced that this multitude of interests and concerns did not bear its secret in itself, and they have felt that apart from this secret the common round must be stale, flat, and unprofitable. What was required was some link that would attach the familiar humdrum to some profounder level of being and, in so doing, give unity and significance to what must otherwise remain both meaningless and confused. On the other hand, it was not as if the humdrum needed no more than to be thus related to its profounder background, in order to satisfy heart's desire; for there has ever been some sense, not merely of something lacking which needs to be supplied, but also of something wrong which needs to be put right.

Life as men familiarly know it has been felt to be not merely incomplete but also out of joint, so that no unification of experience is conceivable, nor any expansion of it profitable, unless there be at the same time a transformation and a renewal.

Now it is always in this double reference that men have spoken of revelation. If we look broadly at the history of religion, we see that what is believed to be revealed is always some clue to a deeper significance of the human situation than appears upon its surface, and at the same time a way of easement or deliverance from the evil of that situation. It is here that the distinction falls between what revelation alone can do for us and all other and lesser aids and enlightenments. As Dr. Tillich says:

The word "revelation" has been used traditionally to mean the manifestation of something hidden which cannot be approached through ordinary means of gaining knowledge. . . . Revelation is the manifestation of what concerns us ultimately. The mystery which is revealed is of ultimate concern to us because it is the ground of our being.[1]

But indeed the same point had been as clearly made by Wilhelm Herrmann nearly half a century earlier:

Only that which rescues us from our predicament, only that which lifts us out of the forlorn condition in which we have hitherto stood, makes upon us the impression of being something utterly new, that is, of being a genuine revelation.[2]

The French novelist and playwright Albert Camus has said in one of his books that after all it does not much matter whether the earth goes round the sun or the sun

---

[1] Tillich, *Systematic Theology*, I, 108, 110.
[2] Herrmann, *Der Begriff der Offenbarung*, p. 6.

round the earth, the only really serious question being whether, either way, our life on the earth is worth living. This may perhaps serve for an illustration of what is meant by the distinction between subsidiary concerns and the ultimate concern.

On the other hand, it is not as if, before any revelation were given, the ultimate concern to which it is relevant were already present in the mind. That is not what has been believed. Rather has it been believed that the revelation opened men's eyes to their deep need at the same time as it showed them how that need could be met.[3] Discontent with one's lot does not arise until some glimpse at least of a better lot has been vouchsafed. Where there is no rumour of higher possibilities, the tragic sense of life will not develop. This is something that can be observed at all levels of experience, but for the higher levels we can quote St. Paul's "I had not known sin, but by the law," [4] and Pascal's "Thou wouldst not be seeking Me, hadst thou not already found Me." [5]

Since something of the tragic sense of life is common to the human race, this implies that to all some revelation has been given. To this question of so-called "general" revelation we shall return,[6] but meanwhile let it be said that historians are agreed that at least the *idea* of revelation is present in all cultures and in all religions. Dr. Hendrik Kraemer, in the fine volume on *The Christian Message in*

---

[3] This is a principle which has its analogical reflection on the intra-human level. Dr. Henry Sloane Coffin quotes from Wordsworth: "Every author, as far as he is great and at the same time original, has had the task of creating the taste by which he is to be enjoyed." (*God Confronts Man in History,* p. 35.)

[4] Rom. 7. 7.   [5] *Pensées,* Brunschvicg ed., 555.

[6] See below, pp. 125ff.

a Non-Christian World, which he prepared for the World Missionary Conference at Tambaram in 1938, does indeed propose to divide the religions of the world into two classes —the religions of revelation, in which he includes only Judaism, Christianity, and Islam, and the naturalist religions, which include all the rest. He concedes, however, that "this division does not imply that the second kind of religions is entirely ignorant of revelation. In a more external sense all religions, not excepting the 'primitive' ones, can be called religions of revelation." [7] The concession suffices for our present purpose, but surely it is enough to cast serious doubt on the serviceability of the original division. Dr. Kraemer seems to be somewhat weakly supporting a weak case when he writes:

In these latter religions the centre of gravity does not lie in the fact or notion of revelation; it is a subsidiary notion, introduced because revelation is such an essentially religious concept that no religion whatever can do without it. But revelation is not at all characteristic of them, and moreover, what they consider to be revelation is of a quite different character from what the religions of revelation understand by it.[8]

If the last sentence means only that not until a fully satisfying revelation has been granted, as we believe it to have been granted in the Christian Gospel, is the nature of the revealing act fully understood, we should very emphatically agree; but that is not enough to justify Dr. Kraemer's procedure. As was pointed out by several of his critics at the Conference itself,[9] what most deeply differentiates the

[7] Kraemer, *The Christian Message,* p. 142.   [8] *Ibid.,* p. 146.
[9] See, e.g., A. G. Hogg, *The Authority of the Faith* (International Missionary Council Madras Series, Vol. I; London, 1940), p. 125: "Christianity is unique because of the unique *content* of the revelation

different religions from one another, so as to yield a just ground for their classification, is not that some regard themselves as being dependent on revelation while others do not, but rather the wide divergence in what they believe to have been revealed—the various ways of deliverance from our ultimate human exigency which they hold themselves divinely authorised to propose and to mediate to their worshippers.

The exigency itself has commonly been recognised as twofold. There is the evil without and there is the evil within. There are the fated limits and limitations of our human existence, "the slings and arrows of outrageous fortune," accident and pain, transiency and mortality; but in ourselves also there is something out of joint, a perversion or a defilement of being which frustrates all dreams of felicity. The two, however, have usually been regarded as interconnected evils, and at last we have the declaration of St. James that "Desire when it has conceived brings forth sin, and sin when it is full-grown brings forth death." [10] When men have spoken of revelation, they have thought of it as providing some kind of easement of both evils at once. There was an easement of fate, whether by changing it or only by enabling men to rise above it in their minds; but there was also a transformation of man's inward being such as put felicity within his grasp.

It was not, however, as if these changes could be brought about by mere increase of knowledge. The thinkers of the Greek enlightenment might take this view, holding that

---

of which it is the apprehension and product, and to which it bears witness." Cf. also D. G. Moses, *Religious Truth and the Relations between Religions* (Madras, 1950), Part II, chap. iii.

[10] Jas. i. 15.

ignorance is the root of all our trouble and that advancing knowledge is sufficient to mend it; and there are those in our own day who similarly pin their hopes to the forward march of science. Such has not, however, been the general mind of our race. The exactly contrary view of the Preacher that "he that increaseth knowledge increaseth sorrow" [11] no doubt represents rather a reaction against Greek intellectualism than any outlook which preceded it, yet most would have found it no farther from the truth than the other. Revelation was indeed regularly conceived as issuing in knowledge, but this knowledge was always of a practical kind. It was knowledge which concerned our ultimate exigency, and what was given us to know was a way of deliverance from that exigency. It was therefore what we should call "saving" knowledge. Yet it was never that alone, and perhaps it was never that even primarily. For what was held to be given was not merely knowledge of the way of deliverance but the deliverance itself. Even among savage peoples it is believed, not only that the traditional rites are of supranatural or transcendent origin, but also that through them men receive an infusion of *power*—a communication of *mana* such as alone renders them effectual. To mention one other example, the Greek mysteries did indeed communicate knowledge, but it was knowledge of how to achieve union with the God, and it was this union alone that brought about the desired deliverance.

When we now turn from what St. Paul called these ignorant ethnic seekings after God, "if haply they might feel after him and find him," [12] and consider the Biblical view of revelation, it is abundantly clear that what is here

[11] Eccles. 1. 18.   [12] Acts 17. 23, 27.

regarded as revealed is a way of deliverance from our ultimate human exigency, a way of salvation. Moreover, it is
not primarily the knowledge of salvation that is spoken of
as revealed, but the salvation itself. Nor is it enough to say
that what God reveals is not a prescription by which we
may save ourselves, but the knowledge that He Himself
has saved us. The Bible does indeed speak of saving knowledge, but this is no mere knowledge *that,* and no mere
knowledge *about;* it is a knowledge *of.* It is what our
epistemologists call knowledge by acquaintance as distinct
from merely conceptual knowledge. God does not give us
information by communication; He gives us Himself in
communion.

Perhaps one other caveat requires here to be entered.
We must beware of talking as if it were only for the mend-
ing of life's wrongness that man has been aware of the
need for God and for His revelation of Himself. Even if
man were unafflicted by the evil within and the evil without, subject to neither sin nor suffering, he could find no
felicity save in communion with God. His most fundamental need for God thus springs from the very eminence and
dignity of his rank in the created order, from the very
superiority of his understanding, from the very maturity
of his powers. According to the myth of Genesis there was
a self-disclosure of God to Adam and Eve in the Garden
before sin and death entered in through the Fall; though
the Fall made necessary a self-disclosure of another kind.
This is a truth that impressed itself very strongly on the
mind of Dietrich Bonhoeffer during the two years he spent
in prison before being hanged by Hitler's agents, and it is
driven home with what is no doubt an exaggerated, though
at the same time a much-needed, emphasis in the beautiful

volume of his letters which has been published posthu-
mously. From much that he says the following may be
quoted:

I should wish to speak of God not at the limits of life but at
its centre, not in the weaknesses of life but in its strength, and
therefore not in regard to man's death and guilt, but in his life
and in his good. At the limits it seems to me better to keep
silence and to leave the insoluble unsolved. The resurrection-
faith is *not* the "solution" of the problem of death. The "beyond" of God is not the beyond of our powers of knowledge!
The epistemologically transcendent has nothing to do with the
transcendence of God. The Church does not stand at the limits,
where human powers fail, but in the middle of the village.
That is the Old Testament way of it, and in this respect we
read the New Testament far too little in the sense of the Old.[13]

We are to find God in what we know, not in what we do
not know. Not in the unsolved but in the solved questions
does God wish to be apprehended by us. That applies to the
relation of God to scientific knowledge. But it applies also to
the universal human questions of death, suffering and guilt.
. . . Here also God is no stop-gap. Not only at the limits of
human possibility must He be known, but at the centre of
life; in life and not only in death; in health and strength and
not only in sin. The ground of this lies in the revelation of
God in Jesus Christ, who is the centre of life and certainly did
not come to answer unsolved questions.[14]

Bonhoeffer goes even further when he writes in another
letter:

In contrast to the other oriental religions the faith of the Old
Testament is no religion of redemption. Yet Christianity is

[13] Dietrich Bonhoeffer, *Widerstand und Ergebung; Briefe und Auf-
zeichnungen aus der Haft,* Eberhard Bethge, ed. (München, 1952), p.
182.
[14] *Ibid.,* p. 211.

constantly described as a religion of redemption. Does this not contain a cardinal mistake by which Christ is separated from the Old Testament and interpreted in the light of the myths of redemption? To the objection that even in the Old Testament redemption (from Egypt and later from Babylon—as in Deutero-Isaiah) has a decisive significance, I reply that we are here dealing with *historical* redemptions, i.e. on this side of the frontier of death, whereas the redemption myths are everywhere concerned with the overcoming of that frontier. Israel is redeemed from Egypt in order that as God's people it may live on earth in the presence of God. . . . Now it will be said that in Christianity, when the resurrection hope was proclaimed, a genuine religion of redemption arose, and that this fact is determinative. . . . But that hope differs from that of the myths precisely in this, that in a quite new way, and even more pointedly than the Old Testament, it refers man back to his life on earth.[15]

While few will be able to go all the way with Bonhoeffer in this and in other things that are written in the same context, all will surely agree that he has here said something that we must keep in mind as we proceed.

THE GOOD NEWS

We have said that it is not enough to think of God as giving us information by communication, but that we must rather think of Him as giving Himself to us in communion. Two things are implied in this. With the first we were concerned in the foregoing chapter, and we said then that it is one of the points on which there appears a remarkable breadth of agreement in recent discussions about revelation. It is that what is fundamentally revealed is God Himself, not propositions about God. Equally remarkable,

[15] *Ibid.*, p. 226.

however, is the recent agreement on the second, which is this: that God reveals Himself *in action*—in the gracious activity by which He invades the field of human experience and human history which is otherwise but a vain show, empty and drained of meaning. In the sequel we shall have to examine very closely the nature of this relation between revelation and history, but meanwhile we shall stay within the area of fairly general agreement.

The Bible is essentially the story of the acts of God. As has often been pointed out, its most striking difference from the sacred books of all other religions lies in its historical character. Other sacred books are composed mainly of oracles which communicate what profess to be timeless truths about universal being or timeless prescriptions for the conduct of life and worship. But the Bible is mainly a record of what God has done. Those parts of it which are not in a strict sense historiographic are nevertheless placed within a definite historical frame and setting which they presuppose at every point. The Mosaic law differs from other law books in that all its prescriptions presuppose the sealing of a covenant between Yahweh and Israel—a covenant which is conceived as being no part of a universal and timeless relation between God and man, but one which was sealed on Horeb-Sinai on a particular historical occasion. Moreover, when the question is raised about such knowledge of God's law as existed in Israel, or in the world at large, prior to this occasion, the answer is again not given in universal terms but in terms of an earlier covenant when, immediately after the Flood, "God spake unto Noah and to his sons with him, saying, And I, behold, I establish my covenant with you, and with your seed after you." [16]

[16] Gen. 9. 8. See below, pp. 130f.

The Book of Psalms, again, would not usually be classed as a historical book, yet the golden thread running through it all is God's saving action in leading Israel out of Egypt, and into the promised land.

We have heard with our ears, O God, our fathers have told us, what work thou didst in their days, in the times of old. How thou didst drive out the heathen with thy hand. . . .[17]

I have considered the days of old, the years of ancient times. . . . I will remember the works of the Lord. . . . I will meditate also of all thy work, and talk of thy doings. . . . Thou leddest thy people like a flock by the hand of Moses and Aaron.[18]

So also the prophets pronounce their oracles, and St. Paul, thinking of the law and the prophets, writes that the Jews' great blessing is that "unto them were committed the oracles of God"; [19] but these oracles differed from those of Delphi and Dodona, as well as of other Eastern religions, precisely in that they were always concerned with the interpretation of definite and contemporary historical situations. God had indeed spoken, but He had spoken through events: "O my people, remember . . . what happened from Shittim to Gilgal, that you may know the saving acts of the Lord." [20]

In Dr. Temple's words:

It is not the subjective consciousness of the prophets which is primary; it is the facts of which they are conscious—the Exodus, the division of the Kingdom, the rise of Assyria and Babylon, the retreat of Sennacherib, the Captivity and Exile, the Return of the Remnant, the rebuilding of the Temple, the triumph of the Maccabees. It is here, in these great events, that

[17] Ps. 44. 1f.   [18] Ps. 77. 5, 11, 12, 20.
[19] Rom. 3. 1.   [20] Mic. 6. 4–5.

the Lord made bare His arm, and the prophetic consciousness
is first and foremost a consciousness of these facts as mighty
acts of God.[21]

Even more unmistakeably, if that be possible, is the New
Testament revelation a revelation through events. It was
with the announcement of an event that the Christian
movement started. We read in the first chapter of the earliest of the Gospels that

after John was arrested, Jesus came into Galilee proclaiming
the good news of God, and saying, The fullness of time is
come [πεπλήρωται ὁ καιρός], and the reign of God is at hand;
change your minds, and trust in the good news.[22]

And St. Paul echoes this when he writes that God

has made known to us, in all wisdom and understanding, the
mystery of his will, according to his purpose set forth in Christ,
as an administration for the fullness of time [εἰς οἰκονομίαν
τοῦ πληρώματος τῶν καιρῶν] to bring all things to a head in
him. . . .[23]

What all the great philosophies do is to offer us a new
interpretation of old and universal facts. What all the
pagan religions attempt is to set men in a new relation to
the situation in which they have stood from the beginning.
Neither the philosophies nor the religions have any fresh
news to announce, but only a fresh adjustment of knowledge or of behaviour to what is already very old, the un-

---

[21] Baillie and Martin, eds., *Revelation,* p. 96. See also H. Richard
Niebuhr, *The Meaning of Revelation,* p. 46: "Even their private visions
were dated, as 'in the year that King Uzziah died,' even the moral law
was anchored to an historical event, and even God was defined less by
his metaphysical and moral character than by his historical relations,
as the God of Abraham, Isaac and Jacob."

[22] Mark 1. 14f.   [23] Eph. 1. 9f.

changing human situation. But the Christian gospel is news in the strict and proper sense of the word. It is concerned from first to last to announce certain new happenings which place men in a situation in which they have never been before. These happenings are given a definite date—"under Pontius Pilate," or "in the fifteenth year of the reign of Tiberius Caesar, Pontius Pilate being governor of Judaea, and Herod being tetrarch of Galilee, and his brother Philip tetrarch of Iturea."[24] Moreover, they are acts of God accomplished in Jesus Himself—in His advent, in His life and preaching, in His sufferings and death, in His resurrection and exaltation. Jesus did not come like John the Baptist, merely to announce an event which would happen independently of Himself. His own coming was the event of which He spoke. In His coming God came, and in this coming of God to us lies our deliverance from what we have called our ultimate human exigency. Here we may quote Dr. Brunner:

In the time of the Apostles no less than in that of the Old Testament prophets God's revelation was regularly understood as the whole divine action for the salvation of the world, the whole *Heilsgeschichte,* the "deeds of God" which reveal His nature and will, and above all as He in whom all former revelation finds its true meaning and who is therefore its fulfilment, Jesus Christ. The revelation is neither book nor doctrine, but God Himself in His historical self-attestation. Revelation is event. . . .[25]

CHRIST WHO IS OUR LIFE

We have spoken of the twofold nature of the exigency from which we are thus delivered. This is always repre-

---

[24] Luke 3. 1.   [25] Brunner, *Offenbarung und Vernunft,* p. 8.

sented in the New Testament by the concepts of sin and
death, but these are believed to be very closely interrelated.
It is when speaking of his struggles against sin that St. Paul
cries out "Who will deliver me from this body of death?" [26]
Death, he tells us, came into the world "through sin" and
"has spread to all men, because all men have sinned." [27]
And death is "the last enemy to be destroyed." [28] Because
of this close interrelation the word most frequently used
in the New Testament to designate the revealed deliverance is *life* (ζωή). Needless to say, life does not here mean
existence. The word is used in the special and exalted
sense which the Old Testament had already made
familiar. Had it been used in its every-day sense, the saying that "man does not live by bread alone" would have
meant that he had need also of some fats and green vege-
tables, whereas in fact it means that he has need of revelation—of "every word of God." [29] Here are some of the
New Testament instances:

In him was life.[30]
I am come that they might have life.[31]
I am the resurrection, and the life.[32]
I am the way, the truth, and the life.[33]
Christ, who is our life.[34]

That as sin hath reigned unto death, even so might grace
reign through righteousness unto eternal life through Jesus
Christ our Lord.[35]

The promise of life which is in Christ Jesus.[36]

[26] Rom. 7. 24.   [27] Rom. 5. 12.
[28] I Cor. 15. 26.   [29] Deut. 8. 3; Matt. 4. 4; Luke 4.4.
[30] John 1. 4.   [31] John 10. 10.
[32] John 11. 25.   [33] John 14. 6.
[34] Col. 3. 4.   [35] Rom. 5. 21.
[36] II Tim. 1. 1.

[The purpose of God] which is now made manifest by the appearing of our Saviour Jesus Christ, who hath abolished death, and hath brought life and incorruptibility to light through the gospel.[37]

For the life was manifested, and we have seen it, and bear witness, and show unto you that eternal life, which was with the Father, and was manifested unto us.[38]

And this is the record, that God hath given to us eternal life, and this life is in his Son. He that hath the Son hath life, and he that hath not the Son of God hath not life.[39]

And he shewed me a pure river of water of life, clear as crystal, proceeding out of the throne of God and of the Lamb.[40]

Such passages, when taken together, make it quite clear that what is manifested or revealed is life; that this life is the overcoming at once of death and of sin and so the final deliverance from our ultimate human exigency; that Christ is this life; and that He is this life because in Him God Himself was revealed. The two contemporary scholars who have written books specifically on the New Testament conception of revelation make these points very clearly. Dr. E. F. Scott writes:

With Paul, therefore, revelation is inseparable from life. He speaks of Christ sometimes as the Revealer, sometimes as the Life-giver; and the two conceptions belong to each other.[41]

And Dr. Bultmann:

Revelation can only be the gift of life which overcomes death. . . . Revelation is an event that destroys death, not a doctrine that death does not exist. . . . It can easily be demonstrated in detail that the verbs which we translate as "to reveal," as well

---

[37] II Tim. 1. 10.   [38] I John 1. 2.
[39] I John 5. 11f.   [40] Rev. 22. 1.
[41] Scott, *New Testament Idea of Revelation*, p. 157.

as the cognate nouns, do not designate a doctrine which enlightens, but an action of God, i.e. an event, in which certainly there is rooted a knowledge on man's part which may be drawn out, but which may also remain concealed.[42]

THE PRESENCE AND THE GLORY

There is, however, something further to be said. The whole of the New Testament revelation emerges from the events that happened under Pontius Pilate. Yet these events yield promise of a further revelation which they do not themselves comprise. They were such as to make our salvation secure but not yet to put it fully in our hands. They gave full warrant of a deliverance which we do not yet fully enjoy. Hence the New Testament looks forward to a further event, a further *Parousia*, a presence or arrival, of Christ, no longer in his humiliation as "in the form of a servant," [43] but in the fullness of His glory. By His presence among us in the flesh Christ has indeed given us life, but meanwhile this is a hidden life, and not until His final *Parousia* will the veil that now covers it be lifted. The Christian, says St. Paul, has already risen with Christ to a new life, but this life is now "hidden with Christ in God," and only "when Christ, who is our life, shall appear, then shall ye also appear with him in glory." [44] In all that the New Testament has to say about revelation this forward reference prevails, especially in most of the contexts where the phrase "the revelation [ἀποκάλυψις] of Jesus Christ" is employed. St. Paul writes to the Corinthians as to "men who wait for the revelation of our Lord Jesus Christ." [45]

[42] Bultmann, *Der Begriff der Offenbarung im Neuen Testament*, p. 22, note 5.

[43] Phil. 2. 7. [44] Col. 3. 3.

[45] I Cor. 1. 7. Cf. II Thess. 1. 7; I Pet. 1. 7; I Pet. 1. 13.

Indeed as time went on, this word apocalypse, which is the most general word for revelation in New Testament Greek, tended to be used exclusively for that which still waits to be revealed. Yet the point needs clearly to be made that this is not an independent or extra revelation, over and above that which is given in the Gospel history itself. The revelation of what is still to be is contained in the revelation of what has already been, and is nothing else than an elicitation of its inherent promise. Our assurance of the full inheritance derives from the earnest of it which we have already received.[46] Or, in another metaphor, our assurance of the final harvest rests on our having already reaped the first fruits of it in the resurrection of Christ and the gift of the Holy Spirit.

> If Christ has not been raised . . . then your faith is vain . . . But in fact Christ has been raised from the dead, the first-fruits of those who have fallen asleep.[47]
> We who have the first-fruits of the Spirit groan inwardly as we wait for the redemption of our bodies.[48]

The Christian Gospel, we have said, is essentially a story. Not the whole of this story is history. It comprises also, as we might say, a "prologue in heaven" and a "postlude in heaven." Yet neither prologue nor postlude can be conceived otherwise than as an implicate of the history which lies between them.

It was not, however, only the word apocalypse or revelation which tended increasingly to be understood with reference to something that is still to be, but also another word that is closely associated with it throughout the whole Biblical literature—the word *glory*. In the Old Testament

[46] Eph. 1. 11–14; II Cor. 5.5.
[47] I Cor. 15. 14–20.   [48] Rom. 8. 23.

the glory of God means His visible or apprehensible presence in the world, but in the later Judaism of the apocalyptic period it came to be reserved for the promised fullness of His presence in the messianic age.

The glory of God is no longer conceived as an actualized or potential experience in this life, but as an element in the messianic age. This new direction of thought came to stay, and glory slowly became eschatological.[49]

For the New Testament writers the messianic age has already dawned, so that they believe the glory of God to have been already revealed to them in Jesus Christ;[50] yet because the fullness of such revelation must await the final consummation, the conception of glory always has in it this forward reference. Christian theology was afterwards to go further, drawing a formal distinction between "the state of grace" which Christians may now enjoy and "the state of glory" which they shall enjoy hereafter; but already in the New Testament, when the words revelation and glory occur together in the same phrase ("when his glory shall be revealed,"[51] or "a partaker of the glory that shall be revealed"[52]), it is the fuller and final presence of Christ that the writer has in mind.

THE MYSTERY

There is one other New Testament concept that here demands our attention. St. Paul is very fond of speaking of what has been revealed as "a mystery"—"the mystery of the Gospel"[53] or "the mystery of God."[54] The Christian mes-

---

[49] Alan Richardson, ed., *A Theological Word Book of the Bible* (London, 1950), *s.v.* "Presence."

[50] II Cor. 4. 6; John 1. 14; I Pet. 4. 13; I Pet. 5. 1.

[51] I Pet. 4. 3.   [52] I Pet. 5. 1.

[53] Eph. 6. 19.   [54] Col. 2. 2.

sage, he says in one place, is "the revelation of the mystery which was kept secret for long ages but is now disclosed." [55] The word appears once in the discourse of Jesus, where St. Mark reports the saying, "To you has been given the mystery of the kingdom of God." [56] It is, however, doubtful whether the word correctly renders anything that our Lord could have said in His Semitic tongue. It is essentially a Pauline word, and most commentators would agree with Dr. E. F. Scott that in this instance "it has been read back into Jesus' own teaching from the thought of St. Paul." [57] It comes from, and had hitherto been associated almost exclusively with, the so-called mystery cults of the Greek world. It is derived from a root which means to close the mouth or eyes, and which resembles the sound one makes in closing the lips, so that it is cognate with our word "mum," when we say "mum's the word." It therefore meant a secret esoteric doctrine or rite, such as must not be disclosed except to the initiated. Thus in modern secular usage a mystery means a secret which has not been disclosed or an event the explanation of which we do not know. St. Paul, however, uses the word differently, since for him the mystery becomes a mystery only in being disclosed, while at the same time, if it were fully disclosed, it would cease to be a mystery. This Pauline usage has been made much of by the theologians of the Orthodox Church, as by the late Father Bulgakoff when he writes:

Mystery ceases to be a mystery if it is not disclosed or, on the other hand, if it is resolved or exhausted by the process of revelation. It is equally characteristic for a mystery to disclose itself and to remain hidden, for it always remains a mystery

---

[55] Rom. 16. 25.   [56] Mark 4. 11.
[57] Scott, *New Testament Idea of Revelation*, p. 148.

in the process of being disclosed. . . . Revelation, therefore, is of the very nature of Deity. God is a self-disclosing Mystery.[58]

Our examination of New Testament usage thus amply confirms our conclusion that what is revealed, that is, the content of revelation, is not a body of information or of doctrine. It may, however, be asked, whether it quite confirms our further conclusion that what is revealed is God Himself. Have we not rather found the content of revelation variously spoken of as life and salvation and glory and mystery and Jesus the Messiah? Are not these what has been revealed?

The answer surely is that all these are but modal manifestations of one and the same reality, and that that reality is God. When we read of "the revelation of Jesus Christ," what we are to understand is that God Himself is being revealed to us in Him. When we read of the revelation of life,[59] it is the eternal Logos, who from the beginning was with God and was God, that is here spoken of. Similarly it is God who is our salvation; it is God who is the self-disclosing Mystery; and the glory which shall be revealed is nothing but the effulgence of God's own deity—for, as Dr. Scott says, "The word 'glory,' wherever it occurs, might almost be translated by 'divinity.' " [60] For all the plurality of expression, the revealed content remains singular. It is indeed true that where St. Mark reports Jesus as speaking of "the mystery of the kingdom," both St. Matthew and St. Luke transpose the phrase into the plural, making it "the mysteries of the kingdom," and this could be taken to mean that what was revealed was a body of esoteric knowl-

---

[58] Baillie and Martin, eds., *Revelation*, pp. 147f.
[59] As in I John 1. 1–2.
[60] Scott, *New Testament Idea of Revelation*, p. 48.

edge. But the original Marcan phrase is free of any such misunderstanding. It is the kingdom itself that is the mystery, and the kingdom is the presence or *Parousia* of God in Christ.

IV: The Mighty Acts of God

No affirmation runs more broadly throughout recent writing on our subject than that which in the last chapter we were concerned to make, namely, that all revelation is given, not in the form of directly communicated knowledge, but through events occurring in the historical experience of mankind, events which are apprehended by faith as the "mighty acts" of God, and which therefore engender in the mind of man such reflective knowledge of God as it is given him to possess. It is clear that this represents a very radical departure from the traditional ecclesiastical formulation which identified revelation with the written word of Scripture and gave to the action of God in history the revelational status only of being among the things concerning which Scripture informed us. Thus, for instance, Aquinas, having defined the revealed (as distinct from the natural) knowledge of God as resting "upon the authority of Scripture confirmed from heaven by miracles," [1] goes on to subdivide this knowledge into (a) suprarational

---

[1] *Summa contra Gentiles*, I, chap. ix.

information concerning God's nature, (b) information concerning His suprarational works—the Incarnation and its sequel, and (c) information concerning suprarational events to be expected at the end of earthly history.[2] Dr. Barth may be suspected of remaining still more biblicist in the traditional sense than most of the other contemporary writers from which we have been quoting, yet it is clear that the same fundamental change has accomplished itself in his thinking. The following may here be added to the quotations already made from his treatment of the subject:

What has generated Scripture and what Scripture in its turn asserts is something that really and definitively, once and once for all, happened. What happened was . . . that God was with us. . . . He was with us as One like unto ourselves. His word became flesh of our flesh, blood of our blood. His glory was seen here in the depth of our predicament, and only when it was there and then illumined by the glory of the Lord was the deepest depth of that predicament made manifest. . . . That did happen, and that is what the Old Testament as the word of prophecy and the New Testament as the word of fulfilment are concerned to announce, but in both cases as having *happened*—happened conclusively, completely, sufficiently.[3]

It is well known that the general concept under which Dr. Barth works out his theology is that of the Word of God. This Word of God, he teaches, always reaches us in a three-fold form—as preached, as written, and as revealed. In our order of knowledge the preaching comes first, but all Christian preaching is dependent upon the witness of prophet and apostle as handed down to us in Scripture. This prophetic and apostolic witness is, however, in its turn to be distinguished from that which alone is the reve-

[2] *Ibid.*, IV, chap. i.   [3] Barth, *Die kirchliche Dogmatik*, I, 118.

lation itself, and which is essentially event—*geschehene
Offenbarung*. What Scripture does is to recall (*erinnern*)
and attest (*bezeugen*) an event which is prior to and to be
distinguished from its own existence (*"ein von ihrer Existenz verschiedene Geschehensein der Offenbarung Gottes
selber"*).[4] "Revelation is therefore originally and directly
what the Bible and the Church's proclamation are deriva-
tively and mediately—the Word of God." [5]

We must, however, think very carefully what we mean
when we say that revelation is given in the form of events
or historical happenings. For it is not as if all who experience these events and happenings find in them a revelation
of God. The question thus arises as to whether even such
events as are in themselves "mighty acts of God" can
properly be spoken of as revelation if, in fact, there should
be nobody to whom they reveal anything. To take the human analogy, do all my efforts to make myself plain
amount to a real self-disclosure, if none succeeds in grasping what is in my mind? Surely not. We must therefore
say that the receiving is as necessary to a completed act of
revelation as the giving. It is only so far as the action of God
in history is understood as God means it to be understood
that revelation has place at all. The illumination of the
receiving mind is a necessary condition of the divine self-
disclosure. Here again we find general agreement among
contemporary theologians. It is to be noted, for instance,
that it is only the prophetic and apostolic *witness* to the
revelation, and not the illumination of the prophetic and
apostolic minds themselves, that Dr. Barth makes posterior
to the event of revelation. The witness does indeed come
afterwards, but the illumination is an integral part of that

[4] *Ibid.*, p. 118.   [5] *Ibid.*, p. 120.

to which witness is borne. So also Dr. Temple, in a very clear exposition which has been widely quoted, finds revelation to consist, not in event taken by itself, but in what he calls "the intercourse of mind and event" or "the coincidence of event and interpretation." [6] "God guides the process," he writes, "He guides the minds of men; the interaction of the process and the minds which are alike guided by Him is the essence of revelation." [7] Similarly Dr. Brunner has it that "The fact of the illumination necessarily belongs to the process of revelation itself; without it an event is no more revelation than light is light without a seeing and illuminated eye. . . . Jesus Christ is not revelation if He is recognized by nobody as the Christ, any more than He is redeemer if there is nobody whom He redeems." [8]

It will be noticed that Dr. Temple speaks of God as guiding, not only the process of events, but also the minds of men in interpreting these events so as to appreciate their revelatory character. This means that the gracious action of God is behind the response men make to His approach, as well as in the approach itself; and this has been the constant testimony of those who have in fact responded. The prophets and apostles all believed that only by God's

[6] Temple, *Nature, Man and God,* pp. 315f.

[7] *Ibid.,* p. 312. Sometimes, it is true, Temple expresses himself a little differently, saying that "the revelation is chiefly given in objective facts yet it becomes *effectively* revelatory only when that fact is apprehended . . ." (*ibid.,* p. 318). "The essential condition of *effectual* revelation is the coincidence," etc. "Consequently in *effective* revelation two factors must normally be present . . ." (Baillie and Martin, eds., *Revelation,* pp. 107f). (Italics added.) The difference, however, is hardly more than verbal.

[8] Brunner, *Offenbarung und Vernunft,* p. 34. Cf. also Wheeler Robinson, *Redemption and Revelation,* pp. 182–85.

own aid were they enabled to interpret His mighty acts. "Surely," says Amos, "the Lord God will do nothing, but he revealeth his secret unto his servants the prophets." [9] This enablement, this illumination, is what is meant by inspiration. The concept of inspiration is thus the necessary counterpart of the concept of revelation, but its meaning and scope have often been misconceived through its being applied primarily to the prophetic and apostolic witness, and withal their *written* witness, to the revelation, rather than to that illumination of the prophetic and apostolic mind which is an integral part of the revelation to which such witness was borne.

HISTORY AND REVELATION

It is, however, necessary to go somewhat deeper in our analysis. Dr. Temple, it will be remembered, speaks not only of the coincidence but also of the *intercourse* and *interaction* of mind and event; and this conception of interaction must be taken very seriously. When so taken, it implies that the events themselves are in their turn conditioned by the human experience of them. The happenings that compose human history must not for a moment be thought of as a continuum which proceeds independently of their impact upon human minds. Rather is history in its very essence a process of action and reaction between external circumstance and human response. "The idea of events-in-themselves," says Dr. Richard Niebuhr, "like that of things-in-themselves, is an exceedingly difficult one." [10] History consists, says Dr. Dodd, "not merely of occurrences, but of events which are occurrences plus *meaning*"; and some events are "such that the meaning of what hap-

[9] Amos 3. 7.   [10] Niebuhr, *The Meaning of Revelation,* p. 83.

pened is of greater importance, historically speaking, than what happened." [11] We are reminded of the frequently quoted dictum of F. W. Maitland that "The essential matter of history is not what happened but what people thought and said about it." Professor Macmurray has more recently written that

History is concerned with what men have done and why they have done it, and essentially with nothing else. If natural events come in, it is only as the setting of human actions; in so far as they impinge upon men and set the problems with which men have to grapple.[12]

And Mr. Victor Murray: "History deals not with events, but with situations which are of significance to somebody." [13]

We need not here stay to think whether some of these statements go too far, but will take from them only as much as confirms us in the conclusion that the sequence of the revelatory events themselves is conditioned by the interpretation put upon them. Sacred history is no mere record of the external fortunes of those who were concerned in it; it is even in greater measure a record of how they behaved in face of these circumstances. The mighty acts of God of which the Bible speaks are not for the most part of the kind that are called "acts of God" in modern legal codes. On the contrary they were accomplished through human agency. The mighty act in which, above all others, God revealed Himself to the Israelite mind was the leading of

[11] Dodd, *History and the Gospel*, pp. 104f.

[12] John Macmurray in *Freedom, Language and Reality*, Aristotelian Society Supplementary Vol. XXV (London, 1951), p. 4.

[13] A. Victor Murray, *Personal Experience and the Historic Faith* (2d rev. ed.; London, 1954), pp. 8of.

the tribes out of Egypt, through the wilderness, into the promised land; but if this was a story of divine action, so also was it at every point a story of human action. God could not, or rather He would not, have led the Israelites on this pilgrimage, if they had one and all refused to be so led. Moses at least had to accept the divine guidance, and to stand firm against the recalcitrants, if the drama was to be enacted at all. This is part of what was meant when we said that revelation and salvation cannot have place unless the divine intention to reveal and to save is met by a human acceptance of revelation and salvation which is none the less a free act for all that it is divinely inspired. The initiative was always with God. The first move was always His. But His second move depended, as constantly comes out in the narratives, upon the response men were enabled to make to the first. This has been well put by Dr. Dodd who writes of "the pattern of history in which God's covenant with men is established" that

It has two elements: (a) a direction of events, and (b) an interpretation of these events. These two elements interact. The message of the prophets arises out of the course of events which they have experienced, and interprets these events; and because they interpreted them just *so* and not otherwise, the history of God's people after the Exile took *that* form and no other; and so all through. The decisive significance of the interaction is accounted for upon the Biblical postulate that God is *both* the Lord of history *and* the Interpreter of His own action to the mind of man. . . . This total structure of event and interpretation is God's Word to man.[14]

Very similarly Dr. Wheeler Robinson has written of the prophets that

[14] Richardson and Schweitzer, eds., *Biblical Authority for Today,* p. 159.

They find in the migration of Bedouin tribes from Egypt the evidence of the redeeming activity of God, and they find in the deportation of Israelites to Babylon the not less clear evidence of the punitive activity of God, vindicating His moral order. The events themselves are, of course, capable of other explanations, but this was theirs, and their explanation became itself a new event of far-reaching consequence for the subsequent history. Through the actuality of their interpretation of other actualities, God was revealed to their contemporaries and successors.[15]

The same principle applies when we pass from the Old Testament (that is, Covenant) to the New; when we pass from the Word as it came to the prophets to the Word made flesh in Jesus Christ. This is the full and final revelation that gathers up all other revelation into itself. Therefore it is just here, in the story of Him who was both very God and very man, that the interaction of divine and human in the coming of the revelation stands out most clearly. "I am not come of myself," [16] says the Jesus of the Fourth Gospel, and "The words that I speak unto you I speak not of myself; but the Father that dwelleth in me, he doeth the works." [17] Yet this "he doeth" is always matched in His discourse by the "I do." "I do always those things that are pleasing to him." [18] "Therefore doth my Father love me, because I lay down my life, that I might take it again. No man taketh it from me, but I lay it down of myself." [19] If Jesus in His manhood had not accepted the commission from the Father, if it were not so that He could have said, "I seek not mine own will, but the will of him that sent me," [20] the sequence of revelatory events could not have

[15] Robinson, *Redemption and Revelation,* pp. 182f.   [16] John 7. 28.
[17] John 14. 10.   [18] John 8. 29.
[19] John 10. 17f.   [20] John 5. 30.

proceeded. And the action of Jesus in doing the Father's will was in the fullest sense free action. It was action which He was tempted not to take, as the Temptation narratives show. "In all points tempted like as we are, but without sinning," [21] says the author of the Epistle to the Hebrews. Nor was the temptation put aside without struggle and self-discipline, as the same writer goes on to say. "Though he were a Son, yet learned he obedience by the things which he suffered; and being made perfect, he became the author of eternal salvation. . . ." [22] Yet this is not for a moment to be understood as if the Father's enablement was not behind the response as truly as His gracious initiative had been behind the commission. "He that hath sent me is with me; he hath not left me alone." [23] This intercourse of the divine and the human is the very meaning of the Incarnation and, as must presently be brought out more fully, it is in Incarnation that revelation could alone be perfected.

REVELATORY SITUATIONS

Meanwhile, however, we must put a prior question. Is the whole of history, with all the events which it contains, to be regarded as in some degree revelatory in character? Dr. Temple has answered this question with an emphatic affirmative. Not only does he refuse to "draw any sharp distinction between the works of God so as to regard some of these as constituting His self-revelation and the others as offering no such revelation," [24] but he affirms that

Unless all existence is a medium of revelation, no particular revelation is possible. . . . Either all occurrences are in some degree revelation of God, or else there is no such revelation at

---

[21] Heb. 4. 15. [22] Heb. 5. 9.
[23] John 8. 29. [24] Temple, *Nature, Man and God,* p. 304.

all; for the conditions of the possibility of any revelation require that there should be nothing which is not revelation. Only if God is revealed in the rising of the sun in the sky can He be revealed in the rising of a son of man from the dead.[25]

The reason Dr. Temple gives is that the God who reveals Himself even in the most exceptional occurrences is revealed as the ultimate Lord of *all* occurrences, as Himself the supreme and ultimate Reality. He can therefore "make no truce with any suggestion that the world for the most part goes on in its own way while God intervenes now and again with an act of His own." [26]

Dr. Temple, however, goes on at once to say that though God's action in the procession of events for the most part follows a uniform pattern, a pattern apprehended by us as what we call "the uniformity of nature," yet when the occasion is sufficient, He interrupts this uniformity, and that there is an exceptional revelatory quality in these occasional variations, because each of them "is an expression of the divine character in face of critical situations, and not only an episode in the age-long activity of God." [27] It may therefore be "not unnatural or inappropriate that the term revelation should be commonly used with a specialised reference to these occasions." [28] Moreover,

The main field of revelation must always be in the history of men, rather than in the ample spaces of nature, though it is also true that if nature were so severed from God as to offer no revelation of Him at all, it would mean that there was no Being fitly to be called God, and therefore no revelation of Him either in human history or elsewhere.[29]

[25] *Ibid.*, p. 306.
[26] *Ibid.*, p. 304.
[27] *Ibid.*, p. 305.
[28] *Ibid.*, p. 314.
[29] *Ibid.*, p. 305.

It is difficult, however, to rest quite satisfied with this formulation. It would seem that a further distinction must be introduced. All must indeed agree that the system of nature, in its very uniformity, is an expression of the divine Will and Wisdom, and therefore so far reveals the mind of the Creator. "The heavens," cries the Psalmist, "declare the glory of God; and the firmament sheweth his handi-work." [30] "Ever since the creation of the world," cries St. Paul, "the invisible things of him, his eternal power and divinity, have been clearly seen in the things that have been made." [31] We know also that Plato found his main evidence of the reality of God just in such uniformity as he was able to perceive in nature, namely, in the orderliness of the procession of the stars. Thomas Chalmers is quoted as having said that "The uniformity of nature is but an-other name for the faithfulness of God."

All this and more is true, yet we may have our doubts as to whether a uniform sequence of natural events could, taken by itself, have suggested divinity, or been appre-hended by Plato or Chalmers or any one else as the mighty work of God, if God had not at the same time revealed Himself in other and more intimate and more personal ways. The course of nature is above all things impersonal. But God is personal, and a person can reveal Himself only through some kind of personal dealings with other persons. Persons are indeed often called upon to act in impersonal ways. They create systems—mechanical systems, legal sys-tems, all sorts of systems. They leave these systems to "run themselves," providing indeed the sustaining power be-hind them, yet not so as to require fresh consideration at

[30] Ps. 19. 1.   [31] Rom. 1. 20.

each stage in their operation. They are therefore not "personally" in evidence throughout the operation of them, but very much hidden behind them. In this same way the course of nature appears to us as a relatively independent and planted-out system. And the question is whether it could in itself reveal to men the Living God who created and sustains it, if God had not already shown, or did not at the same time show, Himself to them as something more than the Creator and Sustainer of such an impersonal system. The late Professor Bowman answered this question in the negative when he wrote that the apprehension of nature's uniformity forms a "first stabilization of human experience," and added that though without such a stabilisation "religion as we understand it would be impossible," yet "were that stabilization complete, there would be no place for the religious attitude. Religion, therefore, is a product of the fact that, having stabilized his life so far, man finds that he has hardly begun to meet his yearnings after *life*." [32] (It will be remembered how *life*, just in this exalted sense of the word which Professor Bowman's italics are meant to bring out, is what we found the New Testament regarding as the essential content of revelation.) Yet we cannot think Dr. Temple to be right in finding evidence of the incompleteness of the stabilisation in the occasional variations from, or interruption of, the uniformity of nature. That is not, as we shall have reason to see in the immediately following section, how the conception of miracle is to be interpreted. The point rather is that the order of nature, even when regarded as most uniform and even

[32] Archibald Allen Bowman, *Studies in the Philosophy of Religion* (London, 1938), II, 233f.

mechanical in its operations, and perhaps *especially* when it is so regarded, cannot possibly be a self-explanatory system. Dr. F. R. Tennant states this well:

Theism, I submit, must be sufficiently tinged with deism to recognise a settled order, and an order in which the causation is not immediate divine causation. . . . At the same time, theism must zealously maintain Butler's qualification of *relatively* settled. This is where it differs from the deism which assumed or implied that God's eternal plan was achieved, and His creative activity exhausted, in creating the world and impressing upon it a system of static and immutable law, so that He became an absentee or mere spectator, and the world a God-forsaken machine.[33]

MIGHTY ACTS

Side by side with Dr. Temple's statement let us now place Dr. Tillich's. To the former "all occurrences are in some degree revelation of God"; to the latter "there is no reality, thing or event which cannot become the bearer" of revelation. To the former everything is revelatory; to the latter nothing is revelatory in its own right, but anything, from a stone to a person, may *become* the medium of revelation. This it does when it enters into what Dr. Tillich calls "a revelatory constellation," that is, when it is an element in a total situation in which the ultimate mystery of being is revealed. On the other hand, when a *person* enters into such a constellation, he becomes more profoundly revelatory than a stone could ever be, as pointing to more significant and central qualities of the divine; [34]

[33] Tennant, *Miracle and Its Philosophical Presuppositions* (Cambridge, 1925), pp. 5of.

[34] Contrast Alexander Pope's "As full, as perfect, in a hair as heart." (*Essay on Man*, Epistle I, line 276.)

though a stone contributes such qualities as endurance and resistance better than a person could do, as when God is said to be the Rock of Ages.[35]

What then are the constellations which do in fact reveal? They are, says Dr. Tillich, those in which a "miracle" is recognised and received in "ecstasy." He is very much alive to the danger of employing either of these terms, since each has been saddled with so many unfortunate latter-day connotations; "but a word which expresses a genuine experience can only be dropped if a substitute is at hand, and it does not seem that such a substitute has been found." It is, however, doubtful whether he has done wisely in adopting the concept of ecstasy, which properly belongs only to one strand in the history of religion, and in the Western world only to that which takes it rises in the mystery cults of ancient Greece.[36] It is better, surely, to speak of inspiration. Dr. Tillich considers this alternative, but on the whole rejects it, being keenly aware of how on the one hand the word has entirely lost its numinous character in ordinary talk, as when we say, "I've had a sudden inspiration!" and on the other has been made to serve a theological doctrine of Scripture as having been given by dictation or something very like it. "In the last analysis," he writes, "a mechanical or any other form of non-ecstatic doctrine of inspiration is demonic." As to miracle, the word suggests to the modern ear a supernatural interference with the laws of nature, against which it must be said that "the manifestation of the mystery of being does not destroy the structure of being in which it becomes manifest." The proper meaning of the

[35] Tillich, *Systematic Theology,* I, 118f.
[36] Though the word is used of St. Peter's vision in Acts 10. 10, and 11. 5.

word is "that which produces astonishment." Only an extraordinary event can produce astonishment, but there are extraordinary regularities as well as extraordinary irregularities. "While everyday life is an ambiguous mixture of the regular and the irregular, in revelatory constellations the one or the other is experienced in its radical form."

Before proceeding, however, we should note the almost point-for-point correspondence between what Dr. Tillich is here saying and what Dr. H. H. Farmer had written sixteen years earlier in his book, *The World and God*. To speak of all nature and history as mediating revelation is for the latter "almost a contradiction in terms." Revelation is a category of personal relationship and can therefore have place only within a situation in which God speaks personally to the individual soul. Hence

If we speak of a general revelation of God in nature and history, the most we can mean is . . . that God may make any situation, into which any man may come at any time, the medium of His revealing word to the soul. . . . Our position is, then, that wheresoever and whensoever God declares Himself to the individual soul in such wise that He is apprehended as holy will actively present within the immediate situation, asking obedience at all costs and guaranteeing in and through such asking the soul's ultimate succour, there is revelation. . . . It follows from this conception of revelation that not all situations are equally calculated to be a medium of it, though any situation may become such, owing to a peculiar relevancy to the individual's life-history, which it may at any moment assume.[37]

Moreover, Dr. Farmer speaks of the relation of miracle to revelation in exactly the same way as Dr. Tillich:

[37] Farmer, *The World and God*, pp. 85–88.

A miraculous event always enters the religious man's experience as a *revelation* of God. . . . Whatever else it may be, it is an event or complex of events through which a man becomes aware of God as active towards him in and through his personal situation. It is God acting relevantly to a man's individual situation and destiny; speaking through events because He is active in events. . . . Unless an event has this quality in some degree to someone it is not, in the religious sense of the term, a miracle.[38]

The only difference between the two writers is that Dr. Farmer holds that while all miracles are revelations, not all revelations are miracles; since it is only when "the experience of God as personal reaches its maximum concentration" that such a concept is really required.[39]

A miracle literally means an occurrence which causes wonder or astonishment. Where the word appears in our translation of the New Testament, the original has either "mighty works" (δυνάμεις) or "signs and wonders" (σημεῖα καὶ τέρατα). Of these three Greek words only the last could accurately be rendered as "miracles," but it is to be noted that it appears only in the compound phrase, never standing by itself. It is not really the astonishing nature of the occurrences that is emphasised in the New Testament, where Jesus is represented as resisting the temptation to act with a view to causing such astonishment. Moreover He deprecated the prevailing desire for "signs." "And the Pharisees came forth, and began to question with him, seeking of him a sign from heaven, tempting him. And he sighed deeply in his spirit, and saith, Why doth this generation seek after a sign? verily I say unto you, There shall no sign be given unto this genera-

[38] *Ibid.*, pp. 109f.   [39] *Ibid.*, pp. 115-18.

tion." [40] And this is taken up by St. Paul when he writes, "For the Jews require a sign . . . but we preach Christ crucified . . . Christ the power (δύναμιν) of God, and the wisdom of God." [41] It would thus appear that of the three English terms, "miracles," "signs," and "mighty works," representing the three Greek words, it is the last that best suggests to us the New Testament point of view. Dr. Tillich, on the other hand, works throughout with the terms "sign-event" and "miracle"; and he writes that "a genuine miracle is first of all an event which is astonishing, unusual, shaking, without contradicting the rational structure of reality. . . . That which does not shake one by its astonishing character has no revelatory power." But he writes also that a miracle is "in the second place an event which points to the ultimate mystery of being, expressing its relation to us in a definite way"; [42] and surely it is here, rather than in the astonishment, that the true emphasis lies. We shall continue to speak of mighty works.

THE WORD MADE FLESH

Our study has thus led us to the conclusion that revelation is always given us through events; yet not through all events, but only through such as appear as God's mighty works; and through no event in its bare character as occurrence, but only as men are enabled by the Spirit of God to apprehend and receive its revelatory power. With this seems to tally the late Dr. Whitehead's doctrine of special or "epochal" occasions, as when he wrote that "Rational religion appeals to the direct intuition of special occasions and to the elucidating power of its concepts for all occa-

[40] Mark 8. 11–12. Cf. Matt. 12. 39; Luke 11. 29.
[41] I Cor. 1. 22–24.   [42] Tillich, *Systematic Theology*, p. 117.

sions. It arises from that which is special, but it extends to that which is general." [43]

Some difficulty may be felt with this doctrine. It may be said that when the starry heavens declare God's glory and show forth His handiwork, this is hardly a revelation in events or one that is mediated by man's historical experience. Yet even apart from the simple consideration that the units of experienced nature are much more truly to be regarded as "point-events" than as particles having spatial position only, it must be answered that all actual experience of natural objects is part of human history and is determined by particular historical situations. This is perhaps obscured from us by our recollection that a thinker like Plato was able to formulate arguments from the universally observed facts of nature to the reality of God which, if they are valid at all, are as independent as all other scientific hypotheses of any particular historical situation or any wider human experience in which those who read Plato may be sharing. Yet the truth surely is that these arguments were but "succedanea and props" for a thought of God and a discovery of the mystery of being whose source was in a much deeper and richer stratum of experience than scientific observation and hypothesis. So also with the writer of the eighth psalm. He did not argue from the heavens to the existence of a God hitherto unknown. These, as Sir George Adam Smith told us, "are not arguments—they are sacraments," [44] that is, pledges in outward and visible symbol of a personal communion already established. We may even venture to quote Wordsworth:

[43] Alfred North Whitehead, *Religion in the Making* (Cambridge, 1927), p. 32.
[44] Smith, *The Book of Isaiah* (London, 1900), II, 90.

Thanks to the human heart by which we live,
Thanks to its tenderness, its joys, its fears,
To me the meanest flower that blows can give
Thoughts that do often lie too deep for tears.[45]

Dr. Temple and Dr. Tillich, we saw, agree that though there is no kind of event through which revelation may not be given, yet some kinds of event are suited to be more deeply revelatory than others. But they agree, further, that the fullness of revelation can be given only in the life of a person. Dr. Temple gives two reasons for this; first that we, who are ourselves persons, can fully understand only what is personal; and second that God, who is a personal being, cannot adequately reveal Himself in anything other than personality.[46] Moreover, if the person in whom the revelation is made is to be fully adequate to His revealing office, he must be one with the God whom he reveals. Thus we cannot have adequate revelation apart from an Incarnation.[47]

That there has been such an Incarnation is, of course, the very essence of our Christian faith. The fullness of revelation is *only* in Jesus Christ, and in Him all other revelation is comprehended and summed up. "For in him," writes St. Paul, "dwelleth the whole fullness of the Deity bodily, and ye have come to fullness in him." [48] In the Old Testament the commonest phrase expressive of revelation, occurring in fact some four hundred times, is "the word of Jahweh." We read again and again that "The word of Jahweh came [*literally,* was] to Jeremiah" or to some other prophet. It came to him in the form of an in-

---

[45] *Ode on the Intimations of Immortality.*
[46] Temple, *Nature, Man and God,* p. 319.
[47] *Ibid.,* p. 322.   [48] Col. 2. 9f.

terpretation of a contemporary situation or event, and of a challenge to action arising out of that interpretation. But the event of which the New Testament speaks is the appearance of a Person who was Himself the Word of God. "The Word became flesh, and dwelt among us." [49] "Admittedly great," we read in the First Epistle to Timothy, "is the mystery of our religion—He who was manifested in the flesh, vindicated by the Spirit, seen by the angels, preached among the nations, believed in by the world, received into glory." [50] The Word is thus no longer clothed merely in *words,* the words of the prophets, but is clothed in flesh and blood. Yet even the Word as it came to the prophets was understood by the Hebrews in a much more concrete way than it could have been by, for example, the Greeks. The latter contrasted the word with the deed, speech with action, so that the opposition (of λόγος and ἔργον) is fundamental to Greek philosophic thought. But in Hebrew the usual word for "word" also means an action or an event, and "for such thought God's fiat and his effective action are one." [51] God speaks, and it is done. "God said, Let there be light: and there was light." [52] "So shall my word be that goeth forth out of my mouth: it shall not return unto me void, but it shall accomplish that which I please, and it shall prosper in the thing whereto I sent it." [53] Thus we are to some extent prepared for the New Testament affirmation that the Word can be seen and touched as well as heard and read. "The Christian doctrine of the Incarnation of the Logos," writes Dr. Tillich, "includes the

[49] John 1. 14.   [50] I Tim. 3. 16.
[51] J. D. A. Macnicol, "Word and Deed in the Old Testament," *Scottish Journal of Theology,* Vol. 5, No. 3 (September, 1952), p. 247.
[52] Gen. 1. 3.   [53] Isa. 55. 11.

paradox that the Word has become an object of vision and touch." [54] As the Epistle to the Hebrews has it, "God, who in former times spoke in various forms and ways to our fathers in the prophets, has in these days at the end spoken to us in a Son." [55] Or as the First Epistle of John has it, "That which was from the beginning, which we have heard, which we have seen with our eyes, which we have looked upon and our hands have touched, concerning the Word of life—and the life was made manifest and we saw it. . . ." [56]

[54] Tillich, *Systematic Theology*, p. 123.   [55] Heb. 1. 1f.
[56] I John 1. 1f. Worth quoting is Taylor, *The Faith of a Moralist*, II, 122: "To a religion which leaves God more or less aloof in the beyond, to be known only by the instructions and commands which come to us from Him, the teaching or the commandment is the primary thing, and the only importance which the bearer of them need have for us is that he is the conduit through which the communication has reached us. So long as we accept the message he transmits, it is really irrelevant what we believe about his personality. But if a religion really brings God down into the heart of temporality, as working through it, not from outside it only, then it will be the person and life in which the complete interpenetration of the eternal and the temporal has been actualised which is itself the revelation, and to believe will be primarily not to assent to the utterances of a messenger, but to recognise a person in whom the interpenetration of the two 'worlds' has been achieved for what he is."

V: The Response to Revelation

When, at the beginning of our study, we traced the break-up of the medieval conception of revelation in the thought of the seventeenth and eighteenth centuries, we were forced to notice among other things a determined shift of emphasis from the theoretical to the practical. Something of the kind is already present in the writings of the first Reformers, and most of all in Luther. There are frequently quoted words of Melanchthon, spoken in direct criticism of the scholastic theology, that "to know Christ is to know His benefits"; words which are taken up later in the preface to the Augsburg Confession of the Lutheran Church.[1] Among the more free-thinking philosophers of the period from Spinoza to Kant we found the bold affirmation that what revelation does for us is not to increase our knowledge or enlighten our intellects but to give us practical guidance; but such formulations appeared to escape the danger of an identification of religion with

[1] Melanchthon, *Loci theologici, Corpus Reformatorum,* XXI, 85; *Apology for the Augsburg Confession,* II, 101.

philosophy only to land us in its identification with morality. Hence the characteristic attempt of nineteenth-century theologians like Schleiermacher and Ritschl was to avoid both dangers, still insisting with Luther upon the practical concern but conceiving it in a way that could not be accused of mere moralism or of preaching "salvation by works."

These may be half-forgotten controversies, but they have profoundly affected our thought and have left their sublimate in our present discussions. This is to be seen above all in the recurring insistence that, in Dr. Temple's words, "every revelation of God is a demand," [2] or in the words of Dr. Martin Buber, "every revelation is a call and a commission." [3] Of interest also in this connection is Dr. Barth's desire to lead us back to the older, prephilosophic and more Biblical meaning of the word "dogma" as command or ordinance rather than doctrinal proposition (*Lehrsatz*).[4] Taken apart from their context such statements might indeed be understood to mean that what is revealed is only a prescription for action, and so once again to be leaving us stranded in a "struggling, task'd morality." Nothing, however, could be further from their intention. For the demand that is here spoken of is a demand of a very specific kind—it is a demand that we should accept a gift. What God asks of us is not that we should do anything for ourselves but that we should allow all to be done for us by Him. Just because this offer is so stupendous, and we have the taking or leaving of it in our own hands, the demand it

[2] Temple, *Nature, Man and God*, p. 254.
[3] Buber, *Ich und Du* (Leipzig, 1923), p. 127.
[4] Barth, *Die kirchliche Dogmatik*, I, 281, 285.

makes upon our wills is the most solemn to which we can ever be subjected. As Dr. Brunner says:

God is revealed to us as *demanding* us for Himself in that He is revealed as the *Giver*. His willing something *for* us is at the same time a willing something *of* us. He demands us for His love. That is His commandment. It is the New Commandment, but only now is it properly conceived as the commandment of Him who gives before He commands and commands only in giving.[5]

PERSONAL TRUST

With this in mind, and keeping in mind also all that has already been said about the divine bestowal of revelation, we may now proceed to consider the human response to it. The Christian name for this response is faith. This English word, like the Greek and Latin words which it translates, has three possible meanings: fidelity, reliance, and credence; faithfulness, trust, and assent. With the first of these meanings we are not here concerned, but the part played by the other two in the response to revelation has been the subject of much discussion. When revelation is conceived as consisting primarily of communicated truths, faith will inevitably be understood as consisting primarily in assent to these truths; and throughout a great part of Christian history it was so understood. Faith was therefore an exercise of the intellect, though an exercise in which the will also takes part; the will, according to Aquinas, moving the intellect to assent.[6] Thus in the Middle Ages three elements

---

[5] Brunner, *Das Gebot und die Ordnungen; Entwurf einer protestantisch-theologische Ethik* (Tübingen, 1932), p. 102.

[6] *Summa theologica*, II, 2. qu. 2, art. 2.

were distinguished in faith; *notitia, assensus,* and *fiducia;*
understanding, assent, and trust. The two former are
clearly intellectual in nature, but the last is as clearly voli-
tional. In what then does *fiducia* consist? The answer
seems to be that prevailingly, and in spite of certain other
commingled strands of meaning, it is understood as submission to the Church's teaching. Thus the *Catholic En-
cyclopaedia* defines faith as "an act of the understanding,
whereby we firmly hold as true whatever God has revealed," but adds that "though it is itself an act of the
understanding, it requires the influence of the will which
moves the intellect to assent." We read further:

The first step . . . is the investigation and examination of the
credentials of the Church, which often is a painful labour last-
ing for years. . . . The intellectual conviction, however, is not
yet an act of faith. One may hesitate or refuse to take the next
step, which is the "good will to believe." . . . And this leads
to the final act, the act of faith itself: I believe what the Church
teaches, because God has revealed it.[7]

Again, Cardinal Gasparri's *Catholic Catechism* gives the
following definition:

Faith is a supernatural virtue whereby, through the inspiration
and help of God's grace, we believe that what God has revealed and has taught us through the Church is true, not because by the natural light of reason we perceive its intrinsic
truth, but on the authority of God who reveals it, for He can
neither deceive nor be deceived.

And in answer to the question, How is faith lost? we are
told that

[7] *S.v.* "Conversion."

Faith is lost by apostasy or heresy—when, that is, a baptized person repudiates all or some of the truths of faith, or deliberately calls them in question.[8]

There is, however, no doubt that all this betokens a very great intellectualising of the conception of faith which we find in the New Testament. It is true that in the later strata of New Testament thought, in the Pastoral and General Epistles, and perhaps also in the Johannine writings, we can already trace the beginnings of an increased emphasis upon the element of assent. But both the Synoptic Gospels and the letters of St. Paul read very differently. On our Lord's own lips the word faith means primarily trust—trust in God and reliance upon His promises. To the disciples who trembled in the storm He said, "Why are you thus afraid? How is it that you have no faith?" [9] To Jairus, when tidings had been brought him of his daughter's death, He said, "Do not fear; only have faith." [10] And to the father of the epileptic boy, "All things are possible for one who has faith." [11] As for St. Paul, Dr. C. H. Dodd sums up a careful treatment by saying that

for Paul faith is that attitude in which, acknowledging our complete insufficiency for any of the high ends of life, we rely utterly on the sufficiency of God. . . . Nor does it mean belief in a proposition, though doubtless intellectual beliefs are involved when we come to think it out.[12]

[8] Gasparri, *The Catholic Catechism, drawn up by His Eminence Peter Cardinal Gasparri; only authorized English translation, by the Reverend Hugh Pope,* o.p. (London, 1934), pp. 198–200.
[9] Mark 4. 40.   [10] Mark 5. 36.
[11] Mark 9. 23.
[12] C. H. Dodd, *The Epistle of Paul to the Romans* (London and New York, 1932), pp. 15f.

There is equally little doubt that when Luther, in criticism of the teaching of Roman orthodoxy, led men's thoughts back to the Pauline doctrine of justification by faith alone, he was at the same time reverting to a more Pauline understanding of what faith itself is. For him the fiducial element in faith is once again primary, and it is no longer understood as submission to the Church's teaching, nor even as acceptance of revealed doctrine, but as trusting in Christ for our salvation. In later Protestant orthodoxy much of this latter advance tended to be lost, and sometimes the element of assent to dogma came near to being restored to its former prominence. Yet nothing could be better than the answer of the Westminster Shorter Catechism to the question "What is faith in Jesus Christ?" which defines it as "a saving grace, whereby we receive and rest upon him alone for our salvation, as he is offered to us in the gospel." How different that is from the corresponding answer in the Catholic Catechism, which was quoted above! It is also a pleasure to be able to quote as follows from one of the best of the English Puritans, John Flavel of Dartmouth:

That only is saving and justifying faith, which is in all true believers, in none but true believers, and in all true believers at all times. . . .

There be three acts of faith, *assent, acceptance,* and *assurance.* The Papists generally give the essence of saving faith to the first, viz. *assent.* The Lutherans, and some of our own, give it to the last, viz. *assurance.* But it can be neither way so. *Assent* doth not agree only to true believers, or justified persons. *Assurance* agrees to justified persons, and to them only, but not to all justified persons, and that at all times.

Assent is too low to contain the essence of saving faith; it is found in the unregenerate as well as the regenerate, yea in devils as well as men (James ii, 19). It is supposed and included in justifying faith, but it is not itself the justifying or saving act. *Assurance* is as much too high, being found only in some eminent believers, and in them too but at some times. . . .

A true believer may "walk in darkness, and see no light" (Isaiah l, 10). Nay a man must be a believer before he know himself to be so. The *direct act* of faith is before the *reflex act:* so that the justifying act of faith lies neither in *assent* nor in *assurance. Assent* saith, I believe that Christ is, and that he is the Saviour of the elect. *Assurance* saith, I believe and am sure that Christ died for me, and that I shall be saved through him. So that *assent widens* the nature of faith too much, and *assurance* upon the other hand *straitens* it too much. But *acceptance,* which saith, I take Christ in all his offices to be mine, this fits it exactly, and belongs to all true believers, and to none but true believers, and to all true believers at all times. This therefore must be the justifying and saving act of faith. . . .

By saving faith Christ is said to "dwell in our hearts" (Eph. iii, 17). But it is neither by *assent* nor *assurance* but by *acceptance,* and receiving him, that he dwells in our hearts; not by *assent,* for then he would dwell in the unregenerate; nor by *assurance,* for he must dwell in our hearts before we can be assured of it; therefore it is by *acceptance.*[13]

How wholly admirable! In Flavel's own words, "this fits it exactly!" But we shall profit from following his thought a little further. From the fact that there may be acceptance, or, as he also calls it, a "fiducial receiving" of Christ where there is little or no assurance, he draws the conclusion that "there must be many more believers in the world than do

---

[13] Flavel, *The Method of Grace* (as reprinted in *The Whole Works,* 1820), pp. 114f.

think and dare conclude themselves to be such." [14] But can there be *fiducia* without *assensus?* Obviously not. A man cannot embrace Christ's salvation without assenting to the fact that Christ is such as to be able to save.

> The receiving of Christ necessarily implies the assent of the understanding to the truths of Christ revealed in the gospel . . . ; which assent, though it be not in itself saving faith, yet is it the foundation and groundwork of it; it being impossible the soul should receive, and fiducially embrace, what the mind doth not assent unto as true and infallibly certain.[15]

On the other hand, a man may assent to the truths of the gospel without knowing that he does so; and the fact of his assent may be evident to others, even when it is not evident to himself, since men are known by the fruit they bear, and a rotten tree *cannot* bring forth good fruit.

There may be, and often is, a true and sincere *assent* found in the soul that is assaulted with violent atheistical suggestions from Satan, and thereupon questions the truth of it. And this is a very clear evidence of the reality of our assent, that whatever doubts or contrary suggestions there be, yet we dare not in our practice contradict or slight those truths or duties which we are tempted to disbelieve. We are assaulted with atheistical thoughts, and tempted to slight and cast off all fears of sin and practice of religious duties, yet when it comes to the point of practice we dare not commit a known sin, the awe of God is upon us; we dare not omit a known duty, the tie of conscience is found strong enough to hold us close to it. In this case it is plain we do really assent, when we think we do not. A man thinks he doth not love his child, yet carefully provides for him in health, and is full of griefs and fears for him in sickness: why now, so long as I see all fatherly duties performed, and affections to his child's welfare manifested, let him say what

[14] *Ibid.*, p. 126.   [15] *Ibid.*, p. 106.

he will as to the want of love to him, whilst I see this, he must excuse me if I do not believe him, when he saith he has no love for him. Just so is it in this case. A man saith I do not assent to the being, necessity, or excellency of Jesus Christ; yet in the meantime his soul is filled with cares and fears about securing his interest in him, he is found panting and thirsting for him with vehement desires, there is nothing in all the world that would give him such joy as to be well assured of an interest in him. While it is thus with any man, let him say or think what he will of his assent, it is manifest by this he doth truly and heartily assent, and there can be no better proof of it than these real effects produced by it.[16]

Or again, more briefly:

It is therefore the policy of Satan, by injecting or fomenting atheistical thoughts . . . to undermine and destroy the whole work of faith. But God makes his people victorious over them: yea, and even at that time they do assent to the truths of the word, when they think they do not; as appears by their tenderness and fear of sin, their diligence and care of duty. If I discern these things in a Christian's life, he must excuse me if I believe him not, when he saith he does not assent to the truths of the gospel.[17]

Yes, we shall excuse him. And again, how wholly admirable! This is "experimental" Puritanism at its best, and it is spoken explicitly against the teaching of the "Romish Church" which is said to place the essence of saving faith in "a naked assent." [18]

THE RELATION OF TRUST TO ASSENT

It is, however, necessary to define a little more sharply the relation of intellectual assent to faith's response to reve-

[16] *Ibid.,* p. 125.
[17] *Ibid.,* p. 107.   [18] *Ibid.,* p. 128.

lation. Flavel says that faith necessarily implies intellectual beliefs but that these need not be self-conscious. Dr. Dodd, in the passage already quoted, says that intellectual beliefs are involved in faith "when we come to think it out." These are two ways of saying very nearly the same thing, but Dr. Dodd's way of saying it reminds us of the fact that the beliefs are not likely to be explicitly reflected upon, or explicitly formulated and affirmed, until some doubt of them appears. When I trust somebody, or have *fiducia* in him, I am manifestly at the same time believing certain things about him to be true, yet I may find it very difficult to say exactly what these things are—I may even flounder helplessly in the attempt to assign the reasons for my trust. This is why the formal development of dogma, and especially of Christological dogma, hardly got under way until the Christian mission had been confronted with the scepticism of the Greek mind. We are indeed, as many commentators have remarked, already aware of a Hellenistically tinged atmosphere when a New Testament writer says that "he that cometh to God must believe that he is, and that he is a rewarder of them that diligently seek him"; [19] because here two intellectual affirmations implied in the fiducial act are explicitly drawn out and formulated.

The intellectual nature of these affirmations is seen in the fact that they are expressed by means of a noun clause introduced by the words "believe that" ($\pi\iota\sigma\tau\epsilon\acute{v}\omega$ $\ddot{o}\tau\iota$) instead of the usual "believe in" ($\pi\iota\sigma\tau\epsilon\acute{v}\omega$ $\epsilon\grave{\iota}s$ or $\grave{\epsilon}\nu$). As time went on, it became necessary to draw out more and more of the intellectual implications of the Christian commitment, and this usage of the verb "to believe" became increasingly common. Yet it is to be noticed that even in the Apostles'

[19] Heb. 11. 6.

and Nicene Creeds we do not confess our belief *that* certain things are true of God and Christ and the Holy Spirit, but our belief *in* God and Christ and the Holy Spirit. It is πιστεύω εἰς, not ὅτι: *credo in,* not *credo* with an accusative and infinitive. The element of commitment here clearly takes precedence over the element of assent. When, however, we go back to the earliest sources of these creeds in the confessional formulae of the apostolic age itself, this precedence becomes more evident still. As Dr. Oscar Cullmann has shown us, the overwhelming majority of these contained one article only. This article, he explains, appears in two principal forms, "Jesus Christ is Lord" and "Jesus Christ the Son of God," but of these it is the former that is primary; it is not His Lordship that explains His Sonship, but His Sonship that serves to explain His Lordship. "It is the present Lordship of Christ . . . that is the centre of the faith of primitive Christianity." [20] When the early Christians confessed that "Jesus Christ is Lord," they were indeed confessing their belief *that* with the advent, passion, death, resurrection, and exaltation of Christ a new era of history had dawned in which Christ rules as King, the powers of evil have been decisively vanquished, and all things have been made new. They were doing that at least implicitly, and the later creeds were to do it more explicitly, and the later dogmatic pronouncements and theological systems to draw out further implications in an explicit way; but what the early Christians were most explicitly doing was confessing their own trust in the Lordship of Christ, and their acknowledgement of it in every department of their lives.

[20] Cullmann, *Die ersten christlichen Glaubensbekenntnisse* (Zürich, 1943), p. 53.

The reason why, as time went on, the true intellectual implicates of Christian commitment had to be increasingly drawn out, and defined with increasing precision, was the appearance on the scene of those who either denied them or gave them a false turn of meaning. It is true of all ancient peoples that they were not self-consciously aware of the part played by beliefs in their religious life and practice. These lay in their minds unchallenged, and therefore the stimulus was lacking to bring them to the light of specific attention and reflection. Something like this was true of the first generation of Christians, living as they did within an oriental society; but when the Christian mission spread to the Greco-Roman world, it was confronted not only with a variety of religious practices quite foreign to its own, and especially with a polytheistic practice shocking to its Hebrew monotheism, but also with a number of philosophic religions which were intellectually very much aware of their own foundations, and in which everything now seemed to turn on what a man believed. Hence it was forced to define very precisely the beliefs latently contained in its own Christian relation to God, and to set them out in a systematic way. As the late Professor Whitehead put it, "Wherever there is a creed, there is a heretic round the corner or in his grave." [21]

The truth then appears to be that while in simple minds, within a simple and settled society, and in an unsophisticated mental climate, faith may flourish bravely without much drawing out of its intellectual implicates, it is far otherwise with those who, like the Christians within the Roman Empire and like ourselves within the modern

[21] Alfred North Whitehead, *Adventures of Ideas* (Cambridge, 1933), p. 66.

West, are participants in a complex and sophisticated culture. Part of the service rendered to faith by theology is of a
negative and protective kind. When there is no false
doctrine abroad, there is the less need to think out true
doctrine; but since false doctrine, where it exists, inevitably
exercises a disturbing and distorting influence on faith,
there is no way to repair the damage save by thinking out
the true. Yet in such a complex culture theology has also a
more positive service to render. When civilization is sufficiently intricate to raise questions concerning the relation
of church and state, of religion and politics, of religion and
economics, of religion and science, of religion and human
learning, and of religion and art, because each of these
other aspects of the life of society has now attained a separate self-consicousness of its own, then there is no solving
of its problems save by the most arduous theological
thought. No refinement of Christian dogmatic formulation, down even to the omission of the *iota* in *homoiousios,*
but is revelant in one of these two ways to some exigency of
Christian living in a confused society like our own.

The desire which is so manifest among present-day
thinkers to understand faith as personal trust rather than
as assent to doctrine thus betokens no attempt to depreciate
the high importance of sound doctrine in its own place.
Indeed most of those who have given emphatic expression
to this desire are theologians who have devoted their lives
to the elaboration of sound doctrine. We may now hear
what one or two of these have to say. First, this from Dr.
Temple:

The life of faith is not the acceptance of doctrine any more
than the life of the natural man is the acceptance of mathematical equations, or the life of the artist is the acceptance of

aesthetic canons. . . . Faith is not the holding of correct doctrines, but personal fellowship with the living God. Correct doctrine will both express this, assist it and issue from it; incorrect doctrine will misrepresent this and hinder or prevent it. Doctrine is of an importance too great to be exaggerated, but its place is secondary, not primary. I do not believe in any creed, but I use certain creeds to express, to conserve, and to deepen my belief in God.[22]

Much of the difficulty that men find in accepting traditional Christianity is due to their belief that what is chiefly asked of them is intellectual assent to certain propositions. They may not regard these as untrue, but they refuse to affirm them until they have worked them out for themselves; they see no sufficient reason for taking them on trust. In revolt against what seems to them an exaggeration of formalism they desire a "formless faith," though they often agree, when challenged, that this would be hard to transmit from generation to generation or to propagate through the world. But if the revelation is given in events, and supremely in the historical Person of Christ, this difficulty is avoided. For an event is not vague or indefinite, even if no number of theories exhaust its significance, and men who differ profoundly in their theories of the Atonement may kneel together in penitence and gratitude at the foot of the cross.[23]

This from Dr. A. G. Hebert:

The fundamental confusion with regard to dogma is the assumption that revelation consists in guaranteed doctrines or beliefs. . . . Scholasticism, accepting the inheritance of Aristotle, identified faith with correct beliefs. The main body of Roman Catholic theology still makes this assumption; in the Anglican Church the Tractarians took it for granted, and much Anglo-Catholic theology has continued to do so. The

[22] Temple, *Nature, Man and God*, pp. 321f.
[23] Baillie and Martin, eds., *Revelation*, p. 105.

one great theologian of the nineteenth century who saw
through the assumption was Frederick Denison Maurice, that
seer and prophet of the future whose importance has never
yet been fully recognized.[24]

And this from Dr. Brunner:

In the New Testament faith is a relationship of person to
Person, man's trustful obedience towards the God who graciously comes to meet him. Revelation is here "truth as encounter," and faith is knowledge as encounter. But in the secret
process of transmutation by which the early Christian became
the ancient Catholic Church, revelation became doctrine and
faith doctrinal belief. A believer is now no longer, as in the
New Testament, one who has been seized and transformed by
Jesus Christ, but one who accepts what the Church offers him
as divinely revealed doctrine on the ground that either the
Bible or the Church's doctrinal jurisdiction constitutes an authority to which one must submit as a matter of course.[25]

In the Reformation this Catholic conception of faith was
recognized to be a misunderstanding of the New Testament
meaning of the word, and the Biblical understanding of faith
was reinstated. . . . Faith is now again understood as trustful
obedience, and revelation as God's action in Jesus Christ. But
now for a second time in her history the Church's desire for
security made her take the wrong and fateful turning. . . .
There was a return to the Catholic conception of revelation
. . . and it was not perceived that in this way the real gain
of the Reformers' rediscovery had been brought to naught.[26]

Elsewhere Dr. Brunner describes this shift from the personal to the intellectual understanding of faith as "perhaps
the most fateful occurrence in the whole history of the

[24] Hebert, *Liturgy and Society; The Function of the Church in the
Modern World* (London, 1936), p. 108.
[25] Brunner, *Offenbarung und Vernunft*, p. 9.   [26] *Ibid.*, pp. 1of.

Church." [27] Yet he finds a tendency towards it already developing within the later New Testament period, as in the Epistle of James. "It is only," he writes, "because James gives to faith this meaning, which was wholly foreign to the Apostle Paul, that he comes to reject justification by faith." [28]

Finally, there is Dr. Barth who, however, writes somewhat differently. He insists on distinguishing "the truth of revelation" from doctrinal propositions. The former cannot like the latter be "objectified and depersonalized"— cannot be abstracted from the Person who reveals or from the act of decision on the part of the person who receives it. It is of the essence of the truth of revelation to demand such a decision, and "that is exactly what the Catholic conception of dogma as a doctrinal proposition in fact excludes." [29] Yet on the other hand he can write as follows:

To exclude from faith the element of *notitia* or *assensus,* that is, the element of knowledge, to conceive of faith as pure trust which is intellectually formless or indifferent as to its intellectual form, as trust in no matter what and of no matter what kind, and so to render problematic the object of faith and transfer the reality of it to the believing subject, was a possibility of which we can certainly say . . . that even in the early period of the Reformation none of its responsible leaders took it seriously into consideration for a single moment. For the old Protestantism faith is *fiducia,* and is more than *notitia* and *assensus* in so far as man in faith receives the merciful "Immanuel" which the Word of God pronounces. . . . Faith is faith only in that it is *fiducia,* and *notitia* and *assensus* alone would not yet be faith at all, but merely that *opinio historica*

[27] Brunner, *Wahrheit als Begegnung,* p. 118.
[28] Brunner, *Offenbarung und Vernunft,* p. 38, note 14.
[29] Barth, *Die kirchliche Dogmatik,* I, chap. i, 285.

which even the godless may possess. But how could it be *fiducia* without at the same time, and precisely as *fiducia*, being *notitia* and *assensus* too, *fiducia promissionis*, trust in the mercy of God which as *misericordia promissa* meets us in the objectivity of the Word, which has not only form but the form of Word and therefore also, in the faith which receives it, the form of knowledge, the form of "holding for true"? [30]

The temper here is recognisably different. It is clear from this, and from the rest that Dr. Barth has to say in the same context, that his sympathies in the debate are somewhat differently engaged from the others whom we have cited. Yet there is probably nothing that he says to which these would not agree. None of them desires to extrude the elements of *notitia* and *assensus,* and none would tolerate a formless faith from which these were absent. But they are anxious to establish the primacy of trust as over against assent, so that Dr. Brunner can write boldly that "Faith is not primarily faith in a truth—not even in the truth *that* Jesus is the Son of God; but is primarily trust and obedience towards this Lord and Redeemer Himself, and the fellowship with Him that arises out of this trust." [31] And they are anxious also to affirm that the trust and commitment may be wholehearted before the elements of assent which it implicitly contains are drawn out in a self-conscious way, and even when they are drawn out incorrectly; as was said by John Flavel in 1680.

What is important is that there should be correspondence in all points between our understanding of the revelation that is given and our understanding of the faith that receives it. If what is directly revealed is God Himself rather than truths about God, then faith must be primarily trust

---

[30] *Ibid.*, pp. 246f.   [31] Brunner, *Wahrheit als Begegnung,* p. 105.

rather than assent. If God has revealed Himself in a saving Event, then faith must be a reliance upon the saving power of that Event. If revelation is at the same time an offer and a demand, then faith must be understood as an acceptance of the offer which is at the same time a yielding to the demand.

CREED

Our contention has been that Christian faith (*fides salvifica*) consists essentially in reliance (*fiducia*) upon the revelation of God in Christ, that this reliance necessarily presupposes an acquaintance (*notitia*) with its object [32] and also latently contains an assent (*assensus*) to certain affirmations that can be made about that object, but that there are many variations in the degree to which this latent assent becomes patent in men's minds and these affirmations are explicitly drawn out.

It is, however, equally clear that the more explicitly the affirmations are drawn out, and the more precisely they are formulated, the more do Christians differ concerning them. It is, in fact, not altogether easy to find any theological proposition which would secure the unqualified assent of *all* whom we should acknowledge as our fellow Christians and therefore as having *fides salvifica*. This is why the basis of unity on which some hundred and fifty churches came together at Amsterdam in 1948 to form the World Council of Churches had to be very short and simple. It reads "The World Council of Churches is a fellowship of Churches which accept our Lord Jesus Christ as God and Saviour." Yet there have since been some who have voiced objection even to this, contending that the affirmation

[32] "I know whom I have believed" (II Tim. 1. 12).

"Christ is God" is neither Scriptural nor theologically tolerable unless conjoined in the same breath with the other statement "Christ is man." The question is not whether these are right or wrong, but whether their scruples concerning so apparently simple an affirmation should lead us to doubt whether they are men of faith. Or we may take another example. It might be thought that no man can have faith in God unless at least he assents to the proposition "God exists." And the Epistle to the Hebrews might be quoted again: "he that cometh to God must believe that he is"; [33] a verse which, as was noted above, has been frequently felt to be more Hellenic than Hebraic in its emphasis upon the intellectual implications of faith. Yet Dr. Tillich will not allow the simple statement "God exists." "God does not exist," he says; "He is being-itself beyond essence and existence." [34] "Grave difficulties attend the attempt to speak of God as existing." [35] We think him quite wrong, but again that is not the point; the point is that we should not dream, on the ground of this error, of denying that he trusts in God for his salvation. Such examples, which could of course be multiplied indefinitely, show the difficulty of instancing any propositional truth about which we should ourselves be willing to say, when pressed, that unless it be explicitly affirmed, or if it be explicitly denied, saving faith cannot be present.

As has already been remarked, we do not, in the Apostles' and Nicene Creeds, say "I believe that" but "I believe in." What we are explicitly doing is not therefore affirming the truth of theological propositions, but confessing our trust in God, Father, Son, and Holy Spirit. We are acknowledg-

[33] Heb. 11. 6.
[34] Tillich, *Systematic Theology*, I, 205.   [35] *Ibid.*, p. 236.

ing our reliance upon the Gospel, the Good News that God has come to meet us in Christ. We are reminding ourselves of the events by which our salvation is secured. What is most remarkable about these creeds, when compared with such creeds as other religions have produced, is just their historical character—that they are chiefly concerned with events. As often as we say them, we gather together with that first communion of saints in the Upper Room round the things that transpired in that Holy Land long ago. While the attempt to impose a common theological formulation must defeat its own end and lead only to an increased bitterness of division, the office of the creeds is rather to bring us together in one place. "They were all with one accord in one place . . . and they were all filled with the Holy Spirit." [36]

It must, however, be allowed that the latest of the creeds, the so-called Athanasian Creed, or *Quicunque Vult,* dating from the fifth or sixth century, forms something of an exception. It begins with the statement that "Whosoever wishes to be saved must before everything else hold the catholic faith, which unless a man have kept whole and entire he shall without doubt perish everlastingly. But the catholic faith is this"—and then follows a large number of theological propositions before we reach the conclusion that "This is the catholic faith, which unless a man have faithfully and firmly believed, he shall not be able to be saved." Concerning this Dr. Curtis wrote in his *History of Creeds and Confessions of Faith* that "in the tyrannical stress laid in this latest of . . . . creeds upon the necessity, for salvation, of the faithful acceptance of so large a body of metaphysical and controversial doctrine, there lay an

[36] Acts 2. 1–6.

omen of impending disruption in the household of faith." [37] Yet even here it is to be noted that the phrase which in the first instance introduces this body of doctrine reads "The catholic faith is this, that we *worship* (*veneremur*) one God in a Trinity," and so forth. Though this emphasis on worship as over against assent cannot be said to be retained as the document proceeds, it is none the less comforting to have it at the outset.

We have quoted Dr. Hebert as saying that the English theologian of the nineteenth century who most definitely repudiated the identification of faith with assent to dogma was F. D. Maurice. Let us then hear what Maurice has to say about the Apostles' Creed.

There is actually found at this present day, in every Christian country, a certain document called a Creed. . . . It has lasted through a great many storms and revolutions. . . . It is substantially what it was, to say the very least, sixteen hundred years ago. During that time it has not been lying hid in the closet of some antiquarian. It has been repeated by the peasants and children of the different lands into which it has come. It has been given to them as a record of facts with which they had as much to do as any noble. In most parts of Europe it has been repeated publicly every day in the year; and though it has been thus hawked about, and, as men would say, vulgarised, the most earnest and thoughtful men in different countries, different periods, different stages of civilization, have felt that it connected itself with the most permanent part of their being, that it had to do with each of them personally, and that it was the symbol of that humanity which they shared with their brethren. . . .

[37] William Alexander Curtis, *A History of Creeds and Confessions of Faith in Christendom and Beyond: With Historical Tables* (Edinburgh, 1911), p. 86.

Now a man who has noticed these facts, and has settled it in his mind that, whatever they mean, they must mean something, would certainly wish to inquire into the nature of this document which has been diffused so widely, has lasted so long, and has seemed to so many different persons of so much value. He will find, I think, that it differs from all the digests of doctrines, whether religious or philosophical, which he has ever seen. The form of it is, I believe. That which is believed in is not a certain scheme of divinity, but a name—a Father, who has made the heaven and the earth: His Son, our Lord, who has been conceived, born, and died, and been buried, and gone down into hell, who has ascended, and is at the right hand of God, who will come to judge the world: a Holy Spirit who has established a holy universal Church, who makes men a communion of saints, who is the witness and power whereby they receive forgiveness of sins, who shall quicken their mortal bodies, who enables them to receive everlasting life. The Creed is evidently an act of allegiance or affiance. . . .[38]

Again:

The view which the Liturgy takes of the Creeds is sufficiently evident from the mode of their introduction into it. They are made parts of our worship; acts of allegiance, declarations by the whole congregation of the Name into which each one has been baptized; preparations for prayer; steps to communion. The notion of them as mere collections of dogmas is never once insinuated, is refuted by the whole order of the services.[39]

HIC ET NUNC

There is, however, one further point that must be made concerning the relation of revelation to response. We have seen that the divine act of revelation cannot be said to be

---

[38] Maurice, *The Kingdom of Christ,* 3d ed. (1883), II, 6–8.
[39] *Ibid.,* II, 367.

completed unless it be apprehended as such, just as I cannot be said to have revealed anything to you if you do not at all understand what I have desired to convey. As Dr. Brunner says, "This passage from the divine to the human subject is exactly what is meant by revelation in the Biblical teaching." [40] It follows that God reveals Himself to me only in so far as I apprehend Him. Such apprehension, however, must be a fact of my own present experience or nothing at all, and that is why more than one of the writers whom we have been quoting insist that "all revelation is in the present moment."

We may ask what then becomes of all they have said about revelation being given to us in the events of past history; but the answer is that *through* the past God reveals Himself to me *in* the present. This could not be unless He had revealed Himself to others through that past while for them it was still present. Had there been no contemporary prophetic interpretation of God's dealings with Israel, and no contemporary apostolic interpretation of the Gospel history, I should not at this distance be finding the presence of God in them at all. It is probable that I should never have heard about them, and certain that I should never have understood them. On the other hand, I could not know that God had revealed Himself to the prophets and apostles through these events, unless through His revelation of Himself to them He were now revealing Himself to me. I could know indeed that they claimed to have received such a revelation, but I can know that their claim was justified only if, as I read what they say, I too find myself in the presence of God. There are those who say, "We do not doubt that Isaiah in the Temple or St. Paul

[40] Brunner, *Offenbarung und Vernunft*, p. 34.

on the Damascus road had genuine revelations vouchsafed to them, but that does not help us, since we have been favoured with no such revelations." But we must answer that, precisely in proportion to the strength of their belief that these earlier revelations were genuine, they are now themselves sharers in them, themselves convicted of the truth that was then revealed.

This would hold good even if, as so often in traditional theology, the *truth* revealed were believed to consist in propositional *truths,* and the authenticity of the past revelations believed to be guaranteed by external proofs, such as accompanying miracles and fulfilled predictions whose validity must be evident to all observers; but it holds all the more now that this kind of guarantee carries so little conviction among us. The profounder element in the tradition was always that which pointed to the necessity of *fiducia* for any conviction of the authenticity of revelation, and which found at last definitive expression in Calvin's doctrine of the *testimonium internum Spiritus Sancti.* Calvin indeed still believes himself able "to stop the obstreperous mouths" of unbelievers "by evidence of various kinds" for the divine origin of Scripture, but he is even more emphatic that what Scripture reveals "will not find credence in the hearts of men until it is sealed by the interior witness of the Spirit"; hence "it is necessary that the same Spirit who spoke by the mouth of the prophets should penetrate into our hearts, in order to convince us that they faithfully delivered what was divinely entrusted to them." [41] Similarly we read in the Westminster Confession:

We may be moved and induced by the testimony of the Church to an high and reverend esteem of the holy scripture, and the

[41] *Institutes of the Christian Religion,* I, chap. vii, 4.

heavenliness of the matter, the efficacy of the doctrine, the majesty of the style, the consent of all the parts, the scope of the whole (which is to give glory to God), the full discovery it makes of the only way of man's salvation, the many other incomparable excellencies, and the entire perfection thereof, are arguments whereby it doth abundantly evidence itself to be the word of God; yet, notwithstanding, our full persuasion and assurance of the infallible truth, and divine authority thereof, is from the inward work of the Holy Spirit, bearing witness by and with the word in our hearts.[42]

We should put all that differently today, but what is apposite at this point in our discussion is the insistence that God wills to reveal Himself to me today through and by means of His revelation of Himself in the events of long ago to the prophets and apostles of long ago. Dr. Richard Niebuhr well says of the prophets that "One must look with them and not at them to verify their visions." [43] For in thus looking with them, instead of at them, we become contemporaneous with them as far as their seeing is concerned, and as far as what they saw is concerned. So far as it is given to us we are seeing now what they saw long ago. It profits me nothing to hear St. Paul say, "It pleased God to reveal his Son in me," [44] unless, as I hear him say it, and through his saying it, God is pleased to reveal His Son to me also, so that I also can testify Χριστός ἐν ἐμοί. And here we should at least remind ourselves, though we cannot stay to do more, that just in this involvement of the past in the present many contemporary writers have found the differentiation of the realm of history from the realm of nature. In a natural process what is past is dead and done

---

[42] *The Westminster Confession of Faith,* chap. i, 5.
[43] Niebuhr, *The Meaning of Revelation,* p. 72.   [44] Gal. i. 15.

with, but, as Dr. Tillich says, "the presence of the past in the present" [45] is constitutive of the very nature of a historical process; or, as another writer, Dr. Friedrich Gogarten, is bold enough to put it, "History is something that happens in the present." [46]

What is important to understand is how the corporate and the individual aspects of revelation are related to one another. The Christian revelation was not addressed to a number of disparate individuals, but to a community. Only within the *koinonia* has it any reality. It is in fellowship, and only in fellowship, that God reveals Himself.

For where two or three are gathered together in my name, there am I in the midst of them.[47]

They were all with one accord in one place . . . and they were all filled with the Holy Ghost.[48]

And when they were come, and had gathered the church together, they rehearsed all that God had done with them.[49]

He that loveth his brother abideth in the light. . . . But he that hateth his brother is in darkness.[50]

If we love one another, God dwelleth in us.[51]

On the other hand, the revelation vouchsafed only to the fellowship is capable of authentication only so far as, through the fellowship, it reaches the individual; only so far as, when all are of one accord, the Holy Spirit speaks to each.

---

[45] Tillich, *The Interpretation of History* (New York and London, 1936), p. 257.

[46] Gogarten, *Ich Glaube an den Dreieinigen Gott* (Jena, 1926), p. 83.

[47] Matt. 18. 20.

[48] Acts 2. 1–4.   [49] Acts 14. 27.

[50] I John 1. 10–11.   [51] I John 4. 12.

VI: Scripture and Covenant

Each of the recent writers whom we have cited has been concerned to warn us against any simple identification of the Christian revelation with the contents of the Bible, and each has been well aware that in this respect he was breaking with a long-established tradition. Thus we found Dr. Barth writing that "we do the Bible a misdirected honour, and one unwelcome to itself, if we directly identify it with this Other Thing, the revelation itself," and adding that we so transgress as often as we set up a doctrine of the general and uniform inspiration of Scripture. In the Bible, he went on to say, we have in all cases to do with human attempts to repeat and reproduce the Word of God (as spoken directly by God Himself in Jesus Christ) in human thoughts and words with reference to particular human situations, such as those existing in the Corinthian church between A.D. 50 and A.D. 60. "In the one case *Deus dixit,* but in the other *Paulus dixit;* and these are two different things." [1] We may here add the following from another

[1] Reference *supra,* pp. 34–35.

theologian of the same school, Dr. Heinrich Vogel of Berlin:

The old Protestant theory of verbal inspiration transforms the living Word of God into a sacred text, and in its consequent denial of the human character of Scripture evades and fails to appreciate, not only the possibility of offence, but at the same time the reality of faith.[2]

But each of these writers is much more concerned to define the positive relation of Scripture to revelation than to draw this necessary distinction between them, and it is to this question that we must now turn our attention. We have accepted the view that the completed act of divine revelation consists in the intercourse of event and interpretation. God's revealing activity is recognised by the Christian not only in the mighty acts which He performed for our redemption but in His illumination of the prophetic and apostolic mind. He so chose Israel that He not only led them out of Egypt but also enabled Moses and the prophets to grasp the significance of that exodus. He so loved the world that He not only sent His Son but at the same time enabled the apostles to grasp the significance of that mission. Thus St. Paul says that, while Jesus Christ Himself is its chief cornerstone, the Church is built upon the foundation of the apostles and prophets.[3] After the illumination was the witness. The illumination was integral to that to which witness was borne, but the witness itself came afterwards. There was indeed a spoken witness before there was a written one, but it is with the latter that we are at the moment concerned. The Bible is the written witness to that intercourse of mind and event which is the essence of revelation. According to Dr. Barth, "what Scrip-

[2] Vogel, *Gott in Christo* (Berlin, 1951), p. 139.   [3] Eph. 2. 19–21.

ture does is to recall and attest an event which is prior to and to be distinguished from its own existence." [4]

The witness itself is a human activity and as such fallible. Nevertheless we cannot believe that God, having performed His mighty acts and having illumined the minds of prophet and apostle to understand their true import, left the prophetic and apostolic *testimony* to take care of itself. It were indeed a strange conception of the divine providential activity which would deny that the Biblical writers were divinely assisted in their attempt to communicate to the world the illumination which, for the world's sake, they had themselves received. The same Holy Spirit who had enlightened them unto their own salvation must also have aided their efforts, whether spoken or written, to convey the message of salvation to those whom their words would reach. This is what is meant by the inspiration of Holy Scripture.

THE CLAIM OF INERRANCY

The only point in dispute among Christians has been whether such inspiration is to be regarded as having been "plenary," that is, whether the control exercised by the Holy Spirit was so complete and entire as to overrule all human fallibility, making the writers perfect mouthpieces of the infallible divine self-communication. This is the view of the Roman Church, and it has also been the view prevailing in traditional Protestantism. Within the latter, however, it has been subject to the following weakness. All Christians would agree that the same Holy Spirit who enlightened the minds of prophets and apostles, and who aided the Biblical writers to convey this enlightenment to

[4] Reference *supra*, p. 64.

those who might follow after, has also been present in the Church throughout the ages, aiding its preachers, teachers, and theologians in their own later witness to the same Gospel. The Roman Church holds that this aid has been "plenary," not of course in the case of each individual preacher or teacher, but in the case of the Church's central direction.

We teach and define . . . that the Roman Pontiff, when he speaks *ex cathedra,* that is, when, in discharge of the office of pastor and doctor of all Christians by virtue of his supreme apostolic authority, he defines a doctrine regarding faith or morals to be held by the universal Church, by the divine assistance promised to him in the blessed Peter, is possessed of that infallibility with which the divine Redeemer willed that His Church should be endowed for defining doctrine regarding faith or morals.[5]

Roman theologians contend that the same necessity, which constrains us to believe that God was graciously pleased to provide us with an inerrant Scripture, constrains us also to believe that He has been graciously pleased to provide us in each succeeding age with an inerrant interpreter of Scripture in the person of the Pope; since Scripture itself has been subjected to such an astonishing variety of diverse interpretations, and such a multiplicity of conflicting deductions have been drawn from its utterances, that the former provision without the latter would have been a very partial blessing. The weakness of Protestant orthodoxy has been that it could show no convincing reason for insisting on the plenary nature of the divine assistance to the Scriptural authors while as firmly denying it to the mind of the Church in later days. That is why several of the recent

[5] Decrees of the Vatican Council, *De Ecclesia Christi,* iv.

writers from whom we have been quoting express their
regret that later Protestantism did not rather follow the
tendency occasionally present in Protestant origins to sur-
render the inerrancy of the Bible as well as of the Church.

The traditional teaching, both Roman and Protestant,
was that every part of the Bible is equally, because completely, inerrant. In recent times, however, the attempt has
frequently been made to hold to the inerrancy of some part
of the Bible while surrendering that of the remainder.
Some have drawn the line between the Old Testament and
the New, others between our Lord's own words and all
else. None of these "modernist" expedients can, however,
be regarded as meeting the real difficulties which beset any
doctrine of plenary inspiration.

The dominical utterances, our Lord's own recorded
words, must indeed be held to stand in a category of their
own. In all ages they have been accorded a place by themselves in the Christian mind, even when everything else
in the Bible was regarded as likewise spoken directly by
God, and given at His dictation. Yet any attempt so to
isolate these utterances as to endow them with an infallibility denied to all else must be chastened by two reflections; first that our Lord did not claim to be omniscient
when found in fashion as a man, and second that we know
His words only as reported by the fallible men who were
His disciples. These two reflections are by no means on the
same level, and bear very differently upon the matter now
in hand, yet each has its own relevance. As Dr. Temple
wrote:

Here once more the human element intervenes with all its
limitations, not only those inseparable from the perfect humanity attributed to the Incarnate Lord Himself, but also

those of His faithful but not infallible disciples. And here the purely spiritual authority of the revelation is secured by this removal of what would otherwise have been the almost coercive quality of its divine origin. . . . In the case of Christ as fully as in that of the prophets we have to allow for the occasional character of the recorded utterances. It is true that He refers every occasion to its appropriate principle; but it does not follow that this is the only principle appropriate to some other occasion.[6]

The Christian will believe that he has an infallible authority in the mind of Christ; but he should know also that he has no infallible means of ascertaining its application to given circumstances.[7]

And elsewhere:

The whole reality of this revelation finds its perfect and focal expression in Jesus Himself. It is of supreme importance that it should thus be given in a Person. It is of supreme importance that He wrote no book. It is even of greater importance that there is no single deed or saying of which we can be perfectly sure that He said or did precisely this or that.[8]

In these same contexts, as in many others, Dr. Temple showed himself anxious to make the point, not only that "infallible direction for practical action is not to be had from either Bible or Church or Pope or individual communing with God," but that "in whatever degree reliance upon such infallible direction comes in, spirituality goes out." [9] As to our Lord Himself, "if He had committed Himself to the formulae of conceptual thought, He would

<hr/>

[6] Temple, *Nature, Man and God*, pp. 351f. Cf. Dodd, *The Authority of the Bible*, p. 233.

[7] Temple, *Nature, Man and God*, p. 353.

[8] Baillie and Martin, eds., *Revelation*, p. 114.

[9] Temple, *Nature, Man and God*, p. 353.

have laid a fetter upon human spirits, nor could any formula of action be applicable to all stages of social progress." [10] And as to the Bible, "the message is . . . so inextricably human and divine in one, that no single sentence can be quoted as having the authority of an authentic utterance of the All-Holy God." [11]

Here, then, we have the main respect in which the teaching alike of Romanism and of what Dr. Barth calls "the later Old Protestantism" is challenged by more recent Protestant theology. What is denied is the inerrancy of Scripture, which is the same as to say its plenary inspiration. Sometimes the phrase to be tossed back and forth between the controversialists has been "literal inspiration," but this is an ambiguous phrase and has led to confusion. More commonly the change of outlook has been spoken of as a denial of "verbal inspiration," but this is even more misleading. For on the one hand it is not only in respect of their choice of words to express their thoughts and affirmations that we are unable to claim inerrancy for the Biblical writers, but in respect of their thoughts and affirmations themselves. Nothing could be more artificial than to suppose that these writers were endowed with infallibility in all that they had in mind to say, while the Holy Spirit left them to their own devices as to how they should say it. Hence on the other hand we should have no hesitation in affirming that inspiration extended not only to the thought of the writers, but to the very words they employed in the expression of these thoughts; though in neither case can we say that the inspiration was plenary. If then inspiration is not regarded as plenary, there is no reason why we should not believe in verbal inspiration.

[10] *Ibid.*, p. 352.   [11] *Ibid.*, p. 350.

How shall we separate the thought of St. Paul, or of the author of Deutero-Isaiah, from their language? And—to select only one example—how, as we read Romans 8, verses 31–39, can we fail to feel that the very words are inspired? And indeed St. Paul himself claims no less when he writes:

> We have received, not the spirit of the world, but the Spirit that is from God, in order that we may understand God's gracious dealings with us; and we speak of these in words taught us not by human wisdom but by the Spirit, matching inspired things with inspired words.[12]

Here we can learn from F. D. Maurice:

> When you speak to me of verbal *inspiration,* though I do not like the phrase, though it seems to me to involve a violent—a scarcely grammatical—ellipsis, yet I subscribe most unequivocally to the meaning which I suppose is latent in it. I have no notion of inspired thoughts which do not find for themselves a suitable clothing of words. I can scarcely, even in my mind, separate the language of a writer from his meaning. And I certainly find this difficulty greater in studying a book of the Bible than in studying any other book. . . . But just because I see this link between the inbreathed thought and the spoken word, I must reject as monstrous and heretical the notion of a *dictation.* I call it monstrous and heretical, for I know none more directly at variance with the letter and spirit of Scripture.[13]

All Christians regard the Bible as holy. Holiness is in the first instance an attribute of God alone; He has all holiness in Himself, and from Him all holiness proceeds. Nevertheless the Bible itself applies the adjective much more frequently to what is other than God than it does to God Himself. We read there of holy men, holy angels, holy

---

[12] I Cor. 2. 12f.   [13] Maurice, *The Kingdom of Christ,* II, 194f.

places, holy buildings, holy vessels, holy writings, and a multitude of other holy things. These are holy because of their association with the Holy God. They are, in the constantly recurring phrase, "holy unto the Lord," being the appointed vehicles of his communion with men, and therefore consecrate or set apart to sacred use; and in them all there is an inextricable intermingling of the divine and the creaturely, as there is in the Holy Scriptures of the divine and the human.

The Scriptures are holy because they are the vehicle through which the Gospel is communicated to us. We know nothing of Christ except what comes to us through the Bible, all later communication of Christian knowledge being dependent upon this original record. Hence there is no outside standard by which we can measure the adequacy of the Biblical communication. The judgement we pass upon its details can only be in the light of the whole. To persuade and assure us of its truth we have "the inward work of the Holy Spirit, bearing witness by and with the word in our hearts," [14] but this witness is always "by and with," never independently of, the word. As latter-day Christians we are therefore wholly dependent on the Bible for the light and truth by which we live. Small wonder that we deem it holy!

Consider again the question whether all parts of the Bible are equally inspired. An affirmative answer would mean that the hindrance presented to the divine afflatus by the imperfections of the receiving mind was equal in all cases. This is an answer we cannot give, and we have already found Dr. Barth warning us that such a doctrine of the uniform (*gleichmässig*) inspiration of Scripture has

[14] *The Westminster Confession of Faith*, chap. i, 5.

issued in bad theology. But the question is really an artificial one, as is also the question whether some other books, not included in the canon, are as much inspired as some of the Scriptural ones. Certainly we must say that the inspiration of the Holy Spirit was not denied to later writers, or to later preachers and teachers. It may and must be said that these were dependent upon the Biblical books, and that their inspiration was mediated by the earlier inspiration that came to the Biblical writers; but that does not yield the desired distinction, since many later Biblical writers were dependent upon earlier ones in exactly the same way. That is how a literature always grows. The true distinction between the canonical books and the others is not in the degree of their inspiration but in the purpose for which it was given. The Biblical writers had their own divinely appointed task to perform, and they were given the help necessary to its performance. The task entrusted to later writers was a different one, and they have been given the help necessary for that. Once more we may draw upon the wisdom of F. D. Maurice:

According to the principle of a spiritual kingdom, as we have considered it, inspiration is not a strange anomalous fact; it is the proper law and order of the world; no man ought to write, or speak, or think, except under the acknowledgement of an inspiration. . . . But still you say . . . "Where do you draw the line?" I draw it in this way:—I say, according to the principle of a spiritual kingdom, every man who is doing the work he is set to do, may believe that he is inspired with a power to do that work. . . . The question therefore is not really, Were these men who wrote the Scriptures inspired by God? but, Were they in a certain position and appointed to a certain work? So that we are driven by the argument, as we are driven by the book itself, from that which we read to that which we read of. Was there such a society as that which this book speaks of? Was there such a nation as the Jews? Had they a history? Was there a meaning in that history? Does this book explain to us their history and its meaning? The question of inspiration belongs to these questions—cannot be viewed apart from them.[15]

If the question be put in terms rather of revelation than of inspiration, so that it is asked whether all parts of the Bible are equally the vehicle of revelation, the answer must be given along similar lines. We may safely accept Luther's criterion that the revelatory quality of each part of the Bible is to be judged according to the measure in which it "preaches Christ" (*Christum treibt*); and whatever some have professed in theory, nobody has ever in practice treated all as on the same level in this regard. There are indeed many things in the Bible that seem to have no revelatory quality at all, yet no exercise could be more unprofitable, or indeed more artificial, than to try to make a list of them. We must remind ourselves again that revelation has place only within the relationship between the Holy Spirit of God and the individual human soul. Nothing is the vehicle of revelation for me unless I hear God speaking to me through it. But there is no Christian who hears God speaking to him through every passage in the Bible, so that for each of us there are some passages that are not revelatory at all. Nevertheless it is always our duty to ask ourselves whether the defect may not be in ourselves rather than in the text, whether even here it is not we who are not willing to listen rather than that nothing significant is being said. The thirteenth-century scholars, when they found something in the Aristotelian corpus which seemed

[15] Maurice, *The Kingdom of Christ*, II, pp. 193f.

to them untrue, were always ready to suspect a deficiency of their own understanding rather than a lapse on the part of *il maestro di color che sanno.* They carried their reverence too far, but there are those who might well take a hint from them as regards the reading of Holy Scripture. On the other hand, the intelligent reading of the Bible—"in the Spirit but with the mind also," [16] and the reading of it so as to understand how it *Christum treibt,* depends entirely on our ability to distinguish what is central from what is peripheral; to distinguish its unchanging truth from its clothing in the particular cultural and cosmological preconceptions of the times and places in which it was written; to distinguish also between its essential message and its numerous imperfections—historical inaccuracies, inaccurate or conflicting reports, misquotations or misapplied quotations from the Old Testament in the New, and such like; and withal to distinguish the successive levels of understanding both within the Old Testament and in the transition from that to the New. We must be as frank in our acknowledgement of this as is, for example, Dr. Dodd when, having quoted some passages from Isaiah, he goes on:

Any theory of the inspiration of the Bible which suggests that we should recognize such utterances as authoritative for us stands self-condemned. They are relative to their age. But I think we should say more. They are false and they are wrong. If they were inevitable in that age—and this is a theory which can neither be proved nor disproved—then in so far that age was astray from God. In any case the men who spoke so were imperfectly harmonized with the will of God. [17]

[16] Cf. I Cor. 14. 15.
[17] Dodd, *The Authority of the Bible,* p. 128.

ESSENTIAL REVELATION AND OUTWARD FORM

At this point it is necessary to come to terms with Father Lionel Thornton's considerable work entitled *Revelation and the Modern World*, which appeared in 1950. It is a work of real distinction, containing much that is of value, but it is difficult to extract from it an unambiguous answer to the questions which it raises, and which are the very questions we ourselves have been raising. Its central thesis is the inextricable involvement of every revelation in the particular culture within which it was first given, so that "a supposedly 'essential core' of religion cannot be isolated from the cultural forms with which it is interwoven." [18] All would agree that this involvement and interweaving are such that only through a close study and deep-going sympathetic understanding of these cultural forms is it possible to comprehend the full import of the revelation which they mediate; but Father Thornton goes much further, seeming to say that it is impossible so to distinguish the two as to enable us to hold to the one while in any sense disengaging ourselves from the other. To attempt any such distinction would be to infringe the incarnational principle of the hypostatic union, for "God's self-identification with the minutiae of contemporary life and thought is all of one piece with the doctrine of the incarnation." [19] And with regard to the Bible:

A similar objection may be urged against any attempt to distinguish the essence of revelation from the sacred literature in which it is enshrined. For all such attempts involve us in a process of discrimination by which we sit in judgement on

[18] Thornton, *Revelation and the Modern World*, p. 11.
[19] *Ibid.*, p. 6.

scripture and attempt to decide to what extent and in what degrees its various utterances are inspired.[20]

The Biblical writers

wove the garments in which the theophany is clothed, apart from which it cannot be manifested. For without that external medium of presentation the revelation would simply disappear from our ken, as surely as in a modern scientific romance "the invisible man" was no longer seen when he took off his clothes.[21]

Hence,

If the onion cannot be peeled, we must accept it as it is. Revelation is given in the Whole . . . Scripture as a whole is the Whole with which Revelation is to be identified.[22]

In all this Father Thornton is arguing against what he calls the Liberal Experiment, but he shows himself equally anxious to avoid the imputation of what he calls fundamentalism. In spite, therefore, of having previously deprecated "any attempt to distinguish," he now introduces us to a distinction:

But if we say that Revelation has identity with the vessel in which it is conveyed to us, it is at once obvious that this is that kind of identity which involves distinction, like the identity of the divine and the human in the person of Christ, or again the identity between Christ and the Church.

In evading the Scylla of Liberalism, therefore, we must not make the mistake of falling into the opposite error of bibliolatry or "fundamentalism." Scripture is the Word of God only because, and as, it receives its fulfilment in Christ; and he has other organs for his self-manifestation, such as the Church, the order of creation and that historical complex which is called Christendom.[23]

[20] *Ibid.*, p. 16.
[22] *Ibid.*, p. 130.
[21] *Ibid.*, p. 53.
[23] *Ibid.*, p. 130.

It is, however, difficult to be happy with the apparently unqualified way in which Father Thornton draws the parallel between the relation of the divine to the human in Christ and that of the divine and human elements in the Bible. Christ's was a perfect human nature, and its limitations were only those that attach to the human status as such, whereas the human nature of the Biblical witnesses was imperfect in its own kind. If the analogy were complete, why should we be anxious to avoid bibliolatry any more than Christolatry? Bibliolatry is to be avoided because the Biblical documents are fallible and because we must not worship what is fallible.

The fallibility of Scripture is indeed frankly admitted, as being integral to "the whole method by which God accommodates his greatness to our human frailty."

From this point of view human limitations are God's opportunity. Thus the imperfections of the earthen vessel in which the divine treasure is conveyed are themselves integral to the very nature of revelation itself. In other words human imperfections are constituent elements in a revelation given to sinful creatures. God condescends to the inadequate medium which we have prepared for him.[24]

But if we are forbidden to follow the "liberal" line of distinguishing the essential message of the Bible from the detail of its outward form, and even from "the minutiae of contemporary life and thought," the reader will ask whether the fallibility does not extend to that message itself. The following passage is perhaps intended as an answer to this question:

In rejecting the Liberal doctrine of revelation we inevitably affirmed its opposite. If revelation is not separable from its outward form, then it must be manifested in and through that

[24] *Ibid.*, p. 132.

form. Moreover, so far from hampering theological freedom, the affirmation of this principle secures for theology its necessary safeguards. For example, only so far as the outward form of revelation is vital to faith, can faith itself be subjected to that discipline of knowledge which is indispensable for its healthy functioning. If the outward form does not matter, faith can take refuge in an inner sanctuary to which the critical faculty cannot penetrate.[25]

What are we to make of this? It will be remembered that we found Dr. Temple acknowledging a certain inextricability as between the divine and human elements in the Bible. Its message, he wrote, is "so inextricably human and divine in one, that no single sentence can be quoted as having the authority of an authentic utterance of the All-Holy God." But to say that the divine never reaches us except as intermingled with human elements is not to say that we are wholly unable to disengage the former from the latter, even in cases where the human is not *das ewig Menschliche* but consists of concepts which men at one time framed only afterwards to discard. Yet this is what Father Thornton seems to do, and we are frankly puzzled. Surely, to take only one example but a very obvious one, there is that in the Bible to which we must hold fast in a way to which we cannot hold fast to its pre-Copernican, even pre-Ptolemaic, cosmography of an "up-and-down" and "three-storey" universe; yet to do so is precisely to disentangle the essential revelation from the contemporary thought-form in which alone it could at that time be received. We wish to know what Father Thornton understands by "the scientific scrutiny of the outward form" which "must be freely welcomed by the believer" [26] if it does not involve such a

---

[25] *Ibid.*, p. 129.   [26] *Ibid.*, p. 129.

disentanglement, and also how he would distinguish such
scrutiny from what he so much deprecates—"that process
of discrimination by which we attempt to decide to what
extent and in what degrees its various utterances are inspired." Meanwhile, instead of saying that "Scripture as a
whole is the Whole with which Revelation is to be identified," we shall prefer to say of Scripture, as itself says of
John the Baptist, οὐκ ἦν ἐκεῖνος τὸ φῶς, ἀλλ᾽ ἵνα
μαρτυρήσῃ περὶ τοῦ φωτός. (He was not that light, but
was to bear witness to that light.)

THE NOACHIC COVENANT

Finally, there is the question whether any revelation has
been vouchsafed to those who, being beyond the reach of
Israelite and Christian influence, know nothing of the witness of the prophets and apostles. In raising this question,
we are at once reminded of the traditional distinction between a natural and a revealed knowledge of God with
which we were concerned in our first chapter. Those who
worked with this distinction held that a certain knowledge
of God and things divine did indeed exist outside Judaism
and Christianity, but that such knowledge came by nature
and not by revelation. Nature in this context, however,
could and did mean two different things. First, there was
the tradition, deriving mainly from Plato and Aristotle,
which claimed that knowledge of God could be reached by
deduction from the observed character and behaviour of
external nature, that is, of what St. Thomas Aquinas called
the *sensibilia;* but, as the same thinker well understood,
such knowledge was available only to the few who had the
capacity and opportunity for exact philosophic thought.
On the other hand, however, there was the tradition, de-

riving mainly from the Stoics, which was alive to the fact
that all men everywhere, including those most remote
from the Hebrew and Christian traditions, and including
also many societies which could not possibly be supposed
to have thought out the philosophic arguments, are apparently in possession of some knowledge of God. Hence this
second type of natural theology speaks, not so much of a
knowledge obtained by deduction from the facts of *external* nature, as of a knowledge innate in *human* nature as
such.

Prior to its contact with Greek thought the Hebrew
mind knew nothing of natural theology of either type.
There is indeed a superficial resemblance between the
Stoic teaching that the knowledge and law of God is
graven on all men's minds (*in animo quasi insculpta*) and
the prophecy of Jeremiah in which God says:

But this shall be the covenant that I shall make with the house
of Israel; After those days, saith the Lord, I will put my law in
their inward parts, and write it in their hearts; and will be
their God, and they shall be my people. And they shall teach
no more every man his brother, saying, Know the Lord: for
they shall all know me, from the least of them unto the greatest
of them, saith the Lord: for I will forgive their iniquity, and
I will remember their sin no more.[27]

But the resemblance is no more than superficial. In the
first place, this is not, as for the Stoics, an innate and universal inscription of the law upon the hearts of all men, but
a later inscription of it upon the hearts of one people only.
In the second place, when Jeremiah speaks of the law of
God being written in the hearts of God's people, he does
not mean a knowledge of the law's provisions (which they
already possessed) but such a deep imprinting as ensured

[27] Jer. 31. 33f.; quoted in Hebrews 8. 10–11.

obedience to these provisions; and likewise "knowing the Lord" means the knowledge of obedience and no mere intellectual awareness of God's existence and character.

Within the inter-testamental period, however, the Greek speculations exercised a certain influence on Jewish thought and something of a Jewish natural theology began to be developed. Clear traces of this are to be found in the teaching of St. Paul. He can appeal both to the evidences of God in external nature and to the knowledge of His will implanted in human nature. As to the former, he writes as follows in the first chapter of his Epistle to the Romans:

For the wrath of God is revealed from heaven against all ungodliness and unrighteousness of men who unrighteously suppress the truth, for what is known of God is manifest to them, God himself having made it manifest to them. For the invisible things of him, his eternal power and divinity, are clearly seen, being understood through the things he has made; so that they are without excuse; for though knowing God they did not glorify him as God or give thanks to him, but became profitless in their reasonings and their undiscerning hearts were darkened.[28]

Similarly, in the speech of Paul and Barnabas at Lystra as reported in the Acts of the Apostles, we read that God "in generations gone by allowed all the Gentiles to go their own ways, yet he did not leave himself without witness, doing good and giving you showers of rain from heaven and fruitful seasons." [29]

On the other hand, the influence of the Stoic kind of natural theology comes out no less clearly in the second chapter of the Roman epistle:

[28] Rom. 1. 18–21.   [29] Acts 14. 16f.

For when Gentiles who have not the Law do by nature the things of the Law, though having not the Law, they are a law to themselves. They exhibit the work of the law written in their hearts, their conscience bearing witness, and their thoughts accusing or it may be excusing them. . . .[30]

The language here ("by nature," "conscience," "written in their hearts") is Stoic, as is also that of the speech at Athens reported in the Acts, where a Stoic poet-philosopher is explicitly quoted. But the writing in the heart seems to be understood partly in the Stoic sense and partly in the Hebrew. For it is said that those who have not the Torah not only know by nature some of its prescriptions, but also *do* them by nature. This latter concession, however, is rare in St. Paul. His general position would rather be that the heathen do not obey even when they know, and in numerous passages he denies that they "know God" in that Hebrew sense of knowing which includes communion and obedience.[31]

The only use St. Paul makes of this appeal to the concepts of natural theology is to show that the heathen nations are "without excuse"—as we might say, that they know enough to be better than they are both in morals and in worship. But has he conceded too much? At the beginning of the third chapter he asks and answers this question:

What advantage then has the Jew? Or what is the use of circumcision? Much in every way. But this before all, that they were entrusted with the oracles of God.[32]

Oracle (λόγιον) is a concept inseparably associated with the concept of revelation, so that here we already have more than a hint of the distinction between nature and

[30] Rom. 2. 14f.
[31] E.g., I Thess. 4. 5; I Cor. 1. 21; Gal. 4. 8.   [32] Rom. 3. 1f.

revelation—probably as an echo from late Jewish thought where it was already present. However, neither St. Paul nor any other New Testament writer makes any further use of it.

Intermingled with this application of the concepts of natural theology to the situation of the Gentiles there is, however, in the Apostle's thought another strain which goes back to a much older Hebrew tradition. For he says not only that the heathen do by nature the things of the law and are therefore a law unto themselves, but also that it was God Himself who made manifest to them such knowledge of Him as they possess. This means that the heathen as well as the Jews have been the recipients of some sort of revelation—even if the word used for the showing forth of this knowledge is φανερόω, the word ἀποκαλύπτω being reserved in this context for the showing forth of God's present wrath. But in Hebrew thought revelation is always conceived as being given within a covenant relationship. God makes covenants with men, and in these covenants discloses His ordinances and commandments. The great covenant was that made with Moses on Sinai, when the Torah or Law was given. This earliest version of the Law with its Decalogue was afterwards further developed, as in the Deuteronomic code, but later thought tended to ascribe all such subsequent developments to Moses, so that all were included in the single great covenant made between God and Israel—the covenant in which God declared, "I will be your God and ye shall be my people." At the same time, however, certain earlier covenants began to be spoken of. We read of God's having already made a covenant with Abraham,[33] and the

[33] Gen. 15. 18.

prophet Jeremiah reproaches men with not having obeyed the "words" of this Abrahamitic covenant.[34] But we read also of a covenant made between God and Noah, which was a covenant made, not with Israel or with the Israelites or with the Shemites alone, but with the whole human race before it was divided into the Shemites, the Hamites, and the sons of Japheth.[35] Indeed in the myth of creation the story is carried still further back, behind the Deluge to Adam who is the first man and at the same time man as such. God, we are told, made man in His own image and likeness and gave him commandments and knowledge of Himself. (According to one tradition Seth, Adam's son, was the first to worship God under the name of Yahweh.) [36] In the book of Ecclesiasticus we read:

The Lord created man of the earth . . .
And made them according to his own image . . .
Ears and heart gave he them to understand withal,
He filled them with knowledge and wisdom,
And shewed them good and evil.
He set his eye upon their hearts,
To shew them the majesty of his works.
And they shall praise the name of his holiness
That they may declare the majesty of his works.
He added unto them knowledge,
And gave them a law of life for a heritage.
He made an everlasting covenant with them,
And shewed them his judgements.
Their eyes saw the majesty of his glory;
And their ear heard the glory of his voice.
And he said unto them, Beware of all unrighteousness,
And he gave them commandment, each man concerning his
  neighbour.[37]

[34] Jer. 34. 18.
[36] Gen. 4. 26.
[35] Gen. 9. 8–17.
[37] Ecclus. 17. 1–14.

Here knowledge of God and of His laws is carried back to a covenant made with man when he was first created.

Nevertheless, among these earlier covenants it was that made with the still undivided race after the Deluge, the so-called Noachic covenant, that appears to have been most appealed to in later Judaism.[38] Such knowledge of God and of His laws as the heathen nations were observed to have was believed to be a relic of this original revelation. And this way of accounting for the knowledge of God which the Gentiles possess—a knowledge which, however overlaid and corrupted, is still sufficiently present in their minds to leave them "without excuse"—is really much more germane to St. Paul's thought as a whole than the doctrine of Stoic origin which also influenced his writing at the beginning of the Roman epistle.

A similar preference is very evident among the writers of our own generation whose thought we have here been concerned to review. During the greater part of Christian history the moral and religious consciousness of the nations outside the Hebrew-Christian tradition was, as we have seen, brought within the terms of the distinction between nature and revelation. Recently, however, the old Stoic conception of human nature, conceived as an original and invariable endowment, has been subjected to much dissolving criticism. Human nature is now regarded rather as the product of long historical experience, and whatever in it is good is regarded as the result, reflected in such experience, of God's historical dealings with the soul of man. In this way the current criticism of the older conception of human nature is closely associated with the current theological in-

[38] "The Noachian Covenant is in Jewish tradition the Covenant by virtue of which the fundamental commandments of God are binding upon all men. Thus all men are *endiathekoi*." C. H. Dodd, in Richardson and Schweitzer, eds., *Biblical Authority for Today*, p. 161.

sistence that man can know nothing of God except as God chooses to reveal Himself to him, and that therefore all knowledge of God and of His laws is due to revelation. Thus where older writers contrasted natural with revealed knowledge, most of the writers from whom we have been quoting rather contrast general with specifically Christian revelation. Nor must we think of such general revelation as issuing only in moral knowledge. The impulse to worship is no less clearly manifest beyond the frontiers of the Hebrew-Christian tradition [39] than is the obligation to conform to moral standards, and we can hardly say that one is more or less corrupt than the other. Any such disjunction of moral from religious knowledge and observance was entirely foreign to the thought of St. Paul and should be to ours.

At an earlier stage we said that the sacred books of the ethnic cults differ from the Bible in that the oracles they contain are rarely set within a historic context. These oracles claim to have been revealed. Yet we have claimed that all revelation is given through history. Are we then to say that the claim made for all the contents of such books is false? Was the self-revealing activity of God entirely withdrawn from the souls of those who composed them? We certainly cannot commit ourselves to this negative proposition. We cannot say that God reaches the souls of those whom the Christian Gospel has never reached only through such vestiges of an original "Noachic" revelation as still remains in them, and not through any continuing invasion of their present experience. What we must rather say is that, if indeed there is any measure of authentic insight in the ethnic books, such insight was in fact the fruit

[39] See, e.g., the passage quoted above from Ecclesiasticus.

of God's historical dealings with the souls of the peoples concerned, though these did not themselves realise (as the Hebrews knew so well how to do) the intimacy of their relation to the historical contexts in which they were embedded.

Epilogue: The Challenge of Revelation

It may be well if, before concluding, we should now en-
deavour to approach the whole question of revelation from
a less abstract and more personal point of view than that
which has necessarily engaged our attention in the preced-
ing chapters; and to consider in as realistic a way as possible
the challenge to each one of us individually that is contained in the impingement of the divine upon our daily
life. I shall suggest that this challenge is perfectly summed
up in two words that constantly recur in the Bible, in the
closest association with one another—the words "listen"
and "obey." The Authorized Version uses the word
"hearken" instead of "listen," and it says "hearken diligently" where we should say "listen carefully," but of
course the meaning is the same. To listen and obey—that,
according to the Bible, is what is required of us. Yes, but
what else? The answer is, nothing else. Nothing at all but
to listen carefully for the voice of God, and then to act in
accordance with what we hear. Speaking of faith as the
response to revelation, Dr. Brunner writes in one of his
books that "Faith *is* obedience; nothing else; literally noth-

ing else at all." [1] In another of his books he repeats this, saying that "Faith is obedience, just as in its turn obedience is genuine only when it is faith"; but he now adds that "it is impossible for us to resolve the two words into one," because faith apprehends the indicative of the divine promise, whereas obedience is to the imperative of the divine command, and we are obliged to continue in this back-and-forth movement between indicative and imperative.[2] We may say, then, that in revelation we are addressed in both the indicative and the imperative moods, and that what is required of us is that we should listen to the indicative and obey the imperative. "If thou wilt listen carefully to the voice of the Lord thy God . . . and wilt give ear to his commandments, and keep all his statutes . . . " [3]—how many passages there are in the Bible that begin like that and then go on to say that, if we do so much, God will do all the rest! Men have ever been tempted to think that the important thing in religion is to be punctilious in ritual observances. King Saul said to Samuel, "The people took of the spoil sheep and oxen . . . to sacrifice unto the Lord thy God in Gilgal." But Samuel replied, "Hath the Lord as great delight in burnt offerings and sacrifices, as in obeying the voice of the Lord? Behold, to obey is better than sacrifice, and to listen than the fat of rams." [4]

To listen and to obey, to be alert to whatever God may have to say to us, and then to adjust our lives to what we hear—if that be all that is required of us, we cannot surely say that it is too much to ask. For it means that if we hear nothing, there is nothing that we are expected to do. Surely

[1] Brunner, *Der Mittler* (Tübingen, 1927), "Schluss."
[2] Brunner, *Das Gebot und die Ordnungen* (Tübingen, 1932), p. 68.
[3] Exod. 15. 26.   [4] I Sam. 15. 20–22.

also, if we took this truth to heart, we should live much less troubled and anxious lives than we habitually do. So often we conduct ourselves as if the whole direction of things were in our own hands, as if we had to invent for ourselves the part we are meant to play, as if the whole of human destiny depended upon the exercise of human wit. Small wonder, then, that we enjoy so little calm and peace of mind, that we are so feverish in our activity, that our nerves are overwrought and the muscles of our hearts overstrained. As Wordsworth wrote as long ago as 1798, believing as we do

> That nothing of itself will come,
> But we must still be seeking,

we refuse to "feed this mind of ours/In a wise passiveness." [5] And we are even further from enjoying the experience of the Hebrew prophet, "Thou wilt keep him in perfect peace, whose mind is stayed on thee, because he trusteth in thee." [6]

Ah yes, we may reply, that would indeed be an experience to enjoy, but is it really available to us? It is well enough to invite us to listen, but what if, when we do listen, we hear nothing? That, we may say, is the root of our trouble. Hearken we ever so diligently, we are rewarded only with a stony silence. After all, has not mankind listened attentively enough these thousands of years? How men have searched for God! How that old firmament above us has been scanned on starry nights with all the agony of prayer! How the paths of logic have been scoured and scoured again, if haply they might reveal some sign or hint of the divine reality! And what, we may ask, has been

[5] *Expostulation and Reply.*   [6] Isa. 26. 3.

the result but a tense and oppressive silence? That Sphinx in the Egyptian desert is the true representation of Deity. Upon our stormy questionings it turns its inscrutable, expressionless face; but no one has ever heard it speak. "He *does* nothing," cried Thomas Carlyle to James Anthony Froude. Even a Hebrew psalmist had on occasion the same complaint to make to God: "We do not see our signs, and there is no longer any prophet. . . . Why dost thou hold back thy hand, why dost thou keep thy right hand in thy bosom?" [7]

Many years ago, when I happened to be preaching in a certain university chapel in the United States, a middle-aged man, who proved to be one of the university's legal representatives, came to me after the service and suggested that we take a walk together before luncheon. I have never forgotten what he had to say. "You speak," he said, "of trusting God, of praying to Him and doing His will. But *it's all so one-sided*. We speak to God, we bow down before Him and lift up our hearts to Him. But He never speaks to us. He makes no sign. *It's all so one-sided.*" Nor was it without real understanding and fellow-feeling that I heard him speak thus, for there had been a time when I used to say the same things to myself. For the same reason also I feel keenly that this kind of difficulty must be taken very seriously, and faced quite squarely without any effort at evasion. Pious folk who refuse to face it squarely show only that they are afraid of it, and give the impression that they are not sufficiently sure of their own ground. Or if it be that they tremble like Eli for the Ark of God, they should remind themselves that the Ark is in God's keeping and does not need their protection.

[7] Ps. 74. 9, 11.

I can remember, during my student years in Edinburgh, walking home one frosty midnight from a philosophical discussion on the existence of God, and stopping in my walk to gaze up into the starry sky. Into those deep immensities of space I hurled my despairing question, but it seemed to hit nothing, and no answer came back. I think Joseph Addison must have had a similar experience exactly two centuries before, only that he thought he did get a kind of response and so was able to console himself. I have in mind, of course, his familiar hymn about the stars:

> What though, in solemn silence, all
> Move round the dark terrestrial ball;
> What though no real voice nor sound
> Amid their radiant orbs be found;
> In reason's ear, they all rejoice,
> And utter forth a glorious voice,
> For ever singing, as they shine,
> The hand that made us is divine.[8]

I am not sure that that kind of answer would have altogether satisfied me, even had I received it. Addison lived in the Age of Reason and it was enough for him to hear with reason's ear. I did not indeed expect or desire to hear anything with the ear of flesh—to hear what Addison calls "a real voice or sound"; but I wanted something more than an argument. Yet even an argument I could not at that time get, for I had just been attending a meeting of the university Philosophical Society, and philosophy in the first decades of the twentieth century was not what it had been in the first decades of the eighteenth. The stars that night did not seem to say to me, "The hand that made us is divine."

[8] *Ode,* in *The Spectator,* No. 465 (Saturday, August 23, 1712).

I believe a great many people have that sort of complaint to make against God. If God really exists, they say, why does He not declare Himself more plainly? Why does He not grant us a more unmistakable revelation? Why does He not make one quite certain sign, a sign that he who runs may read, a sign that would for ever put an end to doubt and afford us what we call "fool-proof" evidence not only of His existence but of His will for mankind?

The best comment I can pass on all these questionings is to say how I have now come to feel about my own early questionings. We ask for an unmistakable sign, but I think we have difficulty in saying what would be such a sign. *What sign would we accept?* We do not know what to suggest. St. Paul said, "The Jews require a sign, and the Greeks seek after wisdom"; [9] or, as we might translate it, "The Jews want a miracle and the Greeks want an argument." But Jesus refused to give the Jews what they wanted. St. Mark reports that "he sighed deeply in his spirit, and saith, Why does this generation seek after a sign? verily, I say unto you, There shall no sign be given unto this generation." [10] Again, in the parable of Dives and Lazarus, Jesus explained how useless and unavailing such a sign would be, even were it vouchsafed. Dives pleads with Abraham that Lazarus should be raised from the dead and sent to his father's house; for he believed that if a dead man were to get up and preach to them, they would at last listen and obey. But Abraham replies, "If they hear not Moses and the prophets, neither will they be persuaded, though one rose from the dead." [11] I have now come to ask myself whether that be not true. I have come to ask myself whether

[9] I Cor. 1. 22.
[10] Mark 8. 12.   [11] Luke 16. 31.

God has not already done and is now doing all He can to make His will known to us—short of denying to us that very freedom of inquiry which we are so anxious to conserve for ourselves; and also whether He has not already done and is now doing all He can to make His will *obeyed* by us—short of denying to us that very freedom of will which is the last thing we would ask Him to take away from us. I therefore put the question, What more can He do, whether for our enlightenment or for our salvation, than He did and does in Jesus Christ?

What I now realise very clearly, and am ready to confess, is that much of the trouble in the days when I could not hear God's voice was that I was not really listening. I was partly listening perhaps—giving, as it were, one ear to His commandments; but no promise is made in the Bible to those who partly listen, but only to those who hearken *diligently*. And why did I not thus hearken? It was that there were certain things I did not want to hear. We sometimes speak of people being "conveniently deaf" to human communications, but there is such a thing also as being conveniently deaf towards God; and it is a malady that afflicts us all. There are certain things we just do not want to be told. They would be too inconvenient, too upsetting, too exacting. The readjustment they would involve would be too painful. They would commit us to tasks more difficult and troublesome than we desire to undertake, or they would interfere with certain indulgences we have been allowing ourselves. The rich young man in the Gospels was so eager to get guidance from Jesus that he came to Him running (who says he was not eager?), asking what he must do to inherit eternal life. He had his guidance, but it

was something he did not want to listen to: "Sell whatsoever thou hast, and give to the poor. But when the young
man heard that saying, he went away sorrowful: for he
had great possessions." [12] But he could never again complain of the lack of revelation.

Yet the matter is not always quite so simple as that. The
obstacle of which I have spoken is the first that must be
eliminated, and if it could be eliminated completely, the
others would perhaps no longer give us pause. But other
obstacles there are. I am indeed sure that much of my own
trouble was of the same kind as the rich young man's; but
it was also due in part to certain wrong-headed and illusory
ideas that I had imbibed from the spirit of the age and from
the philosophies that were then in vogue. Our intellectual
sophistication is nowadays so great that it is difficult to
achieve, or to recover, that naked contact of our minds with
the confronting reality out of which true wisdom can alone
be born. Jesus said, "Except ye become as little children. . . ." [13] He said also, "I thank thee, O Father, Lord
of heaven and earth, that thou hast hidden these things
from the wise and learned, and hast revealed them to
νηπίοις"—which we may perhaps translate as "the inno-
cent-minded." [14] Only the innocent and childlike mind
can hearken diligently.

There are thus two questions which I would put to those
(and first to myself) who complain that they are aware of
no divine self-disclosure, or that God does not speak to
them more plainly. First, *Are you sure there is not something which He is plainly saying to you, and to which you*

[12] Matt. 19. 22; cf. Luke 18. 23.
[13] Matt. 18. 3; cf. Mark 10. 15.   [14] Matt. 11. 25; Luke 10. 21.

are not giving ear? Are you really prepared to hear whatever God may have in mind to say to you, no matter what it may turn out to be? Can you honestly say that there is no voice now seeking to make itself heard, and to which you are not attending—perhaps pretending to yourself that you do not hear it? It may be a sense of dissatisfaction with your present way of living, or with some one particular thing in your life, and you are half-unconsciously suppressing it. Or it may be some positive task that is calling you, and you are as it were stopping your ears, because the task is distasteful to you. But it is God who is speaking. That is how He always speaks. That is how revelation always comes. We are not so naive as to suppose that God speaks to us with a physical voice—with what Addison called, not very happily, "a real voice or sound." In our earlier chapters we have seen that revelation always comes in the form of a demand—a demand of which against our own wish and will we are made aware. And we have seen also that it comes to us, not as isolated individuals, but in our fellowship with each other. It is through the claims and needs of our neighbours that God makes His own claim heard.

Then shall they also answer him, saying, Lord, when saw we thee an hungred, or athirst, or a stranger, or naked, or sick, or in prison, and did not minister unto thee?

Then shall he answer them, saying, Verily I say unto you, Inasmuch as ye did it not to one of the least of these, ye did it not to me.[15]

No reply is recorded, for there is none that could be given. If I am aware of any such claim being made upon me, that is God speaking as plainly as He is able. It may be that this is one of the things that even the omnipotent God

[15] Matt. 25. 44f.

cannot do; He cannot, without invading the area of free personality with which He Himself has endowed us, get any further word through to us until we first hearken diligently to the word He is already speaking. We sometimes say of a man that "one can't tell him anything"; but may it not be true of ourselves that God literally cannot tell us anything? At all events, if there is some voice we are hearing and not attending to, we have no right to complain that there is some further voice we are not hearing. It is clearly absurd to be pining for some grand revelation of God's will while we are refusing to attend to this or that small beginning of a revelation that is already unmistakably before us. It may be only "something telling me," as we say, that I am not using my money as I ought—not holding it in stewardship. It may be a recurrent doubt about the strict honesty of some habitual practice. It may be an uncomfortable feeling about a certain indulgence I have been allowing myself. It may even be a secret knowledge that my support of a particular political party or a particular system of philosophy has been grounded in motives of self-interest rather than of honest conviction. I would *like* this or this to be true, and therefore I have been trying to persuade myself that it *is* true, instead of listening to the Truth and allowing it (or shall we not rather say allowing Him—Him who is the Truth) to persuade me. It will perhaps cause no surprise if I confess that in the case of such an one as myself, who have published books, one of the things that prevents me from listening to the truth is my reluctance to revise opinions to which I have already committed myself in print. How far most of us are from the standard set before us by St. Augustine who says to God in his *Confessions:* "He is Thy best servant who looks not so much to hear that from Thee which is conformable to his own will, as rather to conform his will to whatsoever he heareth from Thee." [16] Here also is a solemn warning which was given us nearly two thousand and five hundred years ago, but which is still up to date:

And the word of the Lord came unto Zechariah, saying, Thus speaketh the Lord of hosts, saying, Execute true judgement, and shew mercy and compassions every man to his brother: And oppress not the widow, nor the fatherless, the stranger, nor the poor; and let none of you imagine evil against his brother in your heart. But they refused to hearken, and pulled away the shoulder, and stopped their ears, that they should not hear. Yea, they made their hearts as an adamant stone, lest they should hear the law, and the words which the Lord of hosts hath sent in his spirit by the former prophets: therefore came a great wrath from the Lord of hosts. Therefore it is come to pass that as he cried, and they would not hear; so they cried, and I would not hear, saith the Lord of hosts. [17]

But there is no end to the cleverness of our self-sophistication in this matter. We are never such skilled logicians as when we are trying to find reasons for doing the things we want to do. We are never such eloquent orators as when we are telling ourselves why we should *not* do the things we do not want to do. Here in my own heart I find a Demosthenes, a Cicero, a Pitt in the making—powers that might move mountains if turned to better use! How Sigmund Freud humiliated (and offended) us when he first began telling us that our subconscious rationalization of our prejudices far surpasses in elaboration the conscious use of our reason in the discovery of truth! We do find it quite surprisingly easy to explain out of existence any voice we do not want to hear, any call or any conviction that is

[16] *Confessions*, X, 26.   [17] Zech. 7. 8–13.

unwelcome to us; and almost as easy to reason into existence the voices we do want to hear. And then we reproach
Deity, because no revelation has been given us! It would be
well if, before claiming that no call has come through to
us, we first asked ourselves whether we have not—if the
metaphor will be allowed—been tampering with the receiving apparatus. Then perhaps our search for God will
become rather a search for the thing that is holding us back
from responding to His search for us.

So the second question which I would put is this: *If you
have listened, have you obeyed?* In the Bible that is always
part of the condition: "If thou wilt diligently hearken to
the voice of the Lord thy God . . . and wilt give ear to his
commandments, and keep all his statutes. . . ." That
seems to mean that we can receive no further revelation
until we have not only hearkened to, but also acted upon,
such revelation as we have already received. Nor do I see
that we have any right to grumble at such a dispensation, if
indeed it exists. What right have we to ask for more light
when we are not using the light we already have? It may
be that we do not know what we ask, when we ask for a
full revelation of God. I can remember being pulled up by
a sentence written by the Blessed Henry Suso in A.D. 1335:
"Let not him ask after what is highest in doctrine who yet
stands on what is lowest in a good life." [18] Yet here we are,
clamouring for the mystery of ultimate reality to be laid
bare to us, and not facing up to the little sample of reality
that stares us full in the face—the realities, it may be, of the
family relationships in our own home! This one bit of
God's will for us we do at least know, this immediate duty
that lies so close to our hand. But we do not take to it very
kindly. We find it harsh and unwelcome enough. Is it not

[18] Heinrich Suso, *Das Büchlein der ewigen Weisheit,* chap. xxi.

probable, then, that anything like a full revelation would quite crush us—and quite blind us. "Our God," as we read both in the Old Testament and in the New, "is a consuming fire." [19]

> No angel in the sky
> Can fully bear that sight.[20]

Surely, then, we had better learn to adjust ourselves to the more commonplace demands of our domestic situation before we enquire after that before which the cherubim veil their faces.

> We need not bid, for cloistered cell,
> Our neighbour and our work farewell,
> Nor strive to wind ourselves too high
> For sinful man beneath the sky;
>
> The trivial round, the common task,
> Will furnish all we ought to ask.[21]

We must therefore accept the second condition also: before asking for what we do not hear, we must obey what we do hear. We may remind ourselves of the precept which was "of invaluable service" to Thomas Carlyle when he found himself in what he calls "the fixed Tartarean dark" of mid-nineteenth-century unbelief: "Do the duty which lies nearest to thee, which thou knowest to be a duty. Thy second duty will already have become clearer." [22] Or we may take another passage from St. Augustine's *Confessions:*

Nor had I anything to answer Thee when thou calledst to me, "Awake, thou that sleepest, and arise from the dead, and

[19] Deut. 4. 24; Heb. 12. 29.
[20] Matthew Bridges, "Crown Him with many crowns."
[21] John Keble, "O timely happy!"
[22] Carlyle, *Sartor Resartus,* "The Everlasting Yea."

Christ shall give thee light." And when thou didst on all sides
show me that what Thou saidst was true, I, convicted by the
truth, had nothing at all to answer, but only those dull and
drowsy words, "Anon, anon," "presently," "leave me but a
little." But alack, my "presently, presently" had no present in
it, and my "little while" went on for a long while.[23]

In an earlier chapter Dr. Tillich was quoted as saying
that revelation always means light on our ultimate human
concern. Using slightly different language he writes in
another place that "Revelation is the manifestation of the
mystery of being to the cognitive function of human reason." [24] I have myself confessed that there was a time when
I asked myself whether there had been *any* manifestation
of the mystery, whether *any* light had been given us on our
ultimate human concern; but I have also testified how it
was gradually borne in upon me that in fact more light had
been given me than I had cared to use. Whence came this
light, this challenge of which I was even now aware? I
can give but one answer. The challenge was mediated to
me by my Christian upbringing, and thus through the
Christian Church; but its ultimate source was Jesus Christ.
The voice I heard was indeed "the voice of conscience," but
it was a conscience that had a long history behind it, going
back to the evangelic story. The word that was spoken to
me was ultimately the Word that had been made flesh. In
distinguishing between what he calls original and dependent revelation, Dr. Tillich writes:

The history of revelation indicates that there is a difference
between original and dependent revelations. This is a consequence of the correlative character of revelation. An original
revelation is a revelation which occurs in a constellation that
did not exist before. . . . In a dependent revelation . . . the

---

[23] *Confessions*, VIII, 5.   [24] Tillich, *Systematic Theology*, I, 129.

receiving side changes as new individuals and groups enter the same constellation of revelation. . . . There is continuous revelation in the history of the church, but it is dependent revelation.[25]

In the Old Testament it is often said that no man has ever seen God, and indeed God is made to say, "There shall no man see me and live." [26] This is taken up in the New Testament, but with an addition. St. John says, "No man hath seen God at any time; the only begotten Son, who is in the bosom of the Father, he hath made him known." [27] And, according to St. John, Jesus Himself said in answer to Philip's request to show him the Father, "He that hath seen me hath seen the Father." [28] That is the whole essence of the Christian faith, that Jesus Christ has shown us the Father, that in Him there has been revealed to us all we need to know about our ultimate concern. "All we need to know." There is much that we do not know. Now we know in part, as St. Paul says, and it may sometimes seem to us to be only a very small part. Now we see only, he says again, as in a mirror dimly. The clouds and thick darkness remain, and the light piercing them sometimes seems scant enough. But it is the Light of the World. It is more light than we are ever likely to use. It is enough to see to do our work by, and until we have done our work we have no cause to repine. When our work is done, it is promised that we shall know even as we are known, and that we shall see face to face.

"Then said Evangelist, Keep that Light in your eye, and go directly thereto, so thou shalt see the Gate." [29]

[25] *Ibid.,* p. 126.   [26] Exod. 33. 20.
[27] John 1. 18.   [28] John 14. 9.
[29] John Bunyan, *Pilgrim's Progress.*

Books Contributory to
the Discussion

Frederick Denison Maurice. The Kingdom of Christ; or, Hints on the principles, ordinances, and constitution of the Catholic Church, in letters to a member of the Society of Friends (1838). 3d ed. London, 1883. Vol. II.

Wilhelm Herrmann. Der Begriff der Offenbarung (1887). 2d and rev. ed., reprinted in *Offenbarung und Wunder,* Giessen, 1908.

Clement C. J. Webb. Problems in the Relations of God and Man. London, 1911.

Charles Harold Dodd. The Authority of the Bible. London, 1928.

Rudolf Bultmann. Der Begriff der Offenbarung im Neuen Testament. Tübingen, 1929.

Alfred Ernest Taylor. The Faith of a Moralist. London, 1930. Vol. II, chaps. i–iv.

Frederick Robert Tennant. Philosophical Theology. London, 1930. Vol. II, chap. viii.

Karl Barth. Die kirchliche Dogmatik. München, 1932. 1. bd. There is an English translation by G. T. Thomson, *The Doctrine of the Word of God* (New York, 1936).

William Temple, *abp. of Canterbury*. Nature, Man and God; Being the Gifford lectures delivered in the University of Glasgow in the academical years 1932–1933 and 1933–1934. London, 1934.

Ernest Findlay Scott. The New Testament Idea of Revelation. New York, London, 1935.

Herbert Henry Farmer. The World and God; A Study of Prayer, Providence and Miracle in Christian Experience. London, 1935.

A. G. Hebert. Liturgy and Society; The Function of the Church in the Modern World. London, 1936.

John Baillie and Hugh Martin, eds. Revelation. London, 1937.

Emil Brunner. Wahrheit als Begegnung. Zürich, 1938. There is an English translation by Amandus William Loos, *The Divine-Human Encounter* (London, 1944).

John Martin Creed, The Divinity of Jesus Christ; A Study in the History of Christian Doctrine since Kant. London, 1938. Chap. vi.

Charles Harold Dodd. History and the Gospel. New York, 1938. Chap. i.

Hendrik Kraemer. The Christian Message in a Non-Christian World. With Foreword by the Archbishop of York. London, 1938.

John Baillie. Our Knowledge of God. London, 1939.

Emil Brunner. Offenbarung und Vernunft, die Lehre von der christlichen Glaubenserkenntnis. Zürich, 1941. There is an English translation by Olive Wyon, *Revelation and Reason* (London, 1947).

H. Richard Niebuhr. The Meaning of Revelation. New York, 1946.

Henry Wheeler Robinson. Redemption and Revelation. London, 1942.

Hubert Cunliffe-Jones. The Authority of the Biblical Revelation. London, 1945.

Henry Wheeler Robinson. Inspiration and Revelation in the Old Testament. London, 1946.

Alan Richardson. Christian Apologetics. London, 1947.

Heinz-Horst Schrey. Existenz und Offenbarung. Tübingen, 1947.

Austin Farrer. The Glass of Vision. Westminster [London], 1948.

Reinhold Niebuhr. Faith and History. London, 1949.

Lionel Spencer Thornton. Revelation and the Modern World. London, 1950.

Alan Richardson and Wolfgang Schweitzer, eds. Biblical Authority for Today. London, 1951.

Paul Tillich. Systematic Theology. Chicago, 1951. Vol. I.

Acknowledgements

Acknowledgement is made to the following publishers for permissions to reprint passages quoted at various points throughout this book: George Allen & Unwin, Ltd, for *Mysticism and Logic,* by Bertrand Russell; A. & C. Black Ltd for *The Glass of Vision,* by Austin Farrar, and *Revelation and the Modern World,* by Lionel Thornton; Edinburgh House Press for *The Christian Message in a Non-Christian World* (out of print), by Hendrik Kraemer; Faber and Faber Ltd, for *Revelation,* edited by John Baillie and Hugh Martin; Harper & Brothers for *The World of God,* by Herbert Henry Farmer, and *Idealism as a Philosophy,* by R. F. Alfred Hoernlé; Macmillan & Co. Ltd and St. Martin's Press, Inc., for *Faith of a Moralist,* by Alfred Edward Taylor; Charles Scribner's Sons and T. & T. Clark for *Die kirchliche Dogmatik,* by Karl Barth (Vol. I translated as *Doctrine of the Word of God* by G. T. Thomson); The Student Christian Movement Press and The Westminster Press for *Biblical Authority for Today,* edited by Alan Richardson and Wolfgang Schweitzer; Mrs. William Temple, Macmillan & Co. Ltd, and St. Martin's Press, Inc., for *Nature, Man and God,* by William Temple; and The Westminster Press for *Offenbarung und Vernunft,* by Emil Brunner (translated as *Revelation and Reason* by Olive Wyon, copyright 1946 by W. L. Jenkins, The Westminster Press).